The Best of James Hollis: Wisdom for the Inner Journey

Writings by James Hollis PHD

Compiled and Edited by
Logan Jones, EdD

CHIRON PUBLICATIONS • ASHEVILLE, NORTH CAROLINA

www.ChironPublications.com

Interior and cover design by Danijela Mijailovic
Printed primarily in the United States of America.

ISBN 978-1-63051-976-6 paperback
ISBN 978-1-63051-977-3 hardcover
ISBN 978-1-63051-978-0 electronic
ISBN 978-1-63051-979-7 limited edition paperback

Library of Congress Cataloging-in-Publication Data

Names: Hollis, James, 1940- author. | Jones, Logan, editor.
Title: The best of James Hollis : wisdom for the inner journey / writings by James Hollis, PhD ; compiled and edited by Logan Jones, EdD.
Description: Asheville, North Carolina : Chiron Publications, [2021] | Includes bibliographical references. | Summary: "The Best of James Hollis: Wisdom for the Inner Journey is a collection of excerpts from the writings of James Hollis, PhD, Jungian psychotherapist and author. These selections span across his body of work from The Middle Passage (1993) to Prisms (2021) organized into different topics ranging from the psychological concepts of Carl Jung to the everyday tasks of our living and callings. Hollis's wisdom will challenge readers to find their own path, to be who they are called to be, to take the risks to trust their soul, and thus live a life worthy of their unique gifts. Hollis's writings ask us to live a deeper and more authentic life"— Provided by publisher.
Identifiers: LCCN 2021039269 (print) | LCCN 2021039270 (ebook) | ISBN 9781630519766 (paperback) | ISBN 9781630519773 (hardcover) | ISBN 9781630519780 (ebook)
Subjects: LCSH: Jungian psychology. | Psychoanalysis. | Self-perception.
Classification: LCC BF173 .H724 2021 (print) | LCC BF173 (ebook) | DDC 150.19/54—dc23
LC record available at https://lccn.loc.gov/2021039269
LC ebook record available at https://lccn.loc.gov/2021039270

Books by James Hollis

- *Harold Pinter: The Poetics of Silence*
- *The Middle Passage: From Misery to Meaning at Midlife*
- *Under Saturn's Shadow: The Wounding and Healing of Men*
- *Tracking the Gods: The Place of Myth in Modern Life*
- *Swamplands of the Soul: New Life from Dismal Places*
- *The Eden Project: In Search of the Magical Other*
- *The Archetypal Imagination*
- *Creating a Life: Finding Your Individual Path*
- *On This Journey We Call our Life*
- *Mythologems: Incarnations of the Invisible World*
- *Finding Meaning in the Second Half of Life*
- *Why Good People Do Bad Things: Exploring Our Darker Selves*
- *What Matters Most: Living a More Considered Life*
- *Hauntings: Dispelling the Ghosts that Run Our Lives*
- *Living the Examined Life: Wisdom for the Second Half of the Journey*
- *Living Between Worlds: Finding Personal Resilience in Changing Times*
- *Prisms: Reflections on This Journey We Call Life*

Dedication

To Kelli

Epigraphs

If we fail to live out the portion of eternity given to us,
no one will ever live it.

~ Michael Meade

For we carry our fate with us—and it carries us.

~ Marcus Aurelius

Acknowledgements

Reprinted from *Archetypal Imagination* by James Hollis, Ph.D. by permission of Texas A&M University Press.

Living an Examined Life: Wisdom for the Second Half of the Journey" (c) 2018 James Hollis Ph.D. excerpted with the permission from the Author and the publisher, Sounds True, Inc.
Living Between Worlds: Finding Personal Resilience in Changing Times" (c) 2020 James Hollis Ph.D. excerpted with the permission from the Author and the publisher, Sounds True, Inc.

Excerpts from *The Middle Passage: From Misery to Meaning in Mid-Life* by James Hollis, © 1993 by James Hollis. Used by permission of Inner City Books.
Excerpts from *Under Saturn's Shadow: The Wounding and Healing of Men* by James Hollis, © 1994 by James Hollis. Used by permission of Inner City Books.
Excerpts from *Tracking the Gods: The Place of Myth in Modern Living* by James Hollis, © 1995 by James Hollis. Used by permission of Inner City Books.
Excerpts from *Swamplands of the Soul: New Life in Dismal Places* by James Hollis, © 1996 by James Hollis. Used by permission of Inner City Books.

Table of Contents

Foreword

"It's got to be the going not the getting there that's good." So sang singer-songwriter Harry Chapin (1972, track 2). James Hollis would agree, I think, that the journey itself is more important, more crucial, more life-giving than the destination. The sense of journey—our life as a journey—is intricately woven throughout Hollis's body of work. It is one of the major themes that I found so engaging and provocative. The unfolding of our lives is not so much arriving at a place as it is awakening to the journey we all are summoned to travel. Our journey is our never-ending search for meaning. It unfolds as we wrestle with the questions posed to us by life so we can become our unique selves. In essence, the journey is found in the courage to become who we are meant to become. This living the journey, then, represents the considered life, the examined life. And, in short, is a summary of Hollis's writings.

I first came across the writings of James Hollis some twenty years ago. At the time I was battered and bruised by midlife, by my work as a hospital chaplain and clinical pastoral education (CPE) supervisor where I taught the art of spiritual care to seminary students and clergy. In addition, directing a non-revenue producing department brought on its own unique challenges and stress. There were the endless meetings around budget, FTEs and staffing, patient care

1

issues, and the like. The constant atmosphere of pain and loss, death and grief took its toll. As I now reflect on that time, I see I did not know what to do, where to go, or even who to be. I was well-nigh on to lost. The great question for the second half of life haunted me: What is my soul asking of me now? So I re-entered therapy, began to read the poetry of Rainer Maria Rilke, Rumi, and Mary Oliver, and began to write my own poems. The journey intensified. I was finding myself.

It was during this time I somehow discovered a book by Hollis. Better yet, the book found me. It was, of course, *The Middle Passage*. Little did I know as I read this book where this journey would take me. Mythologist Michael Meade (2012) quotes an old proverb that says, "Before you begin the journey, you own the journey. Once you have begun, the journey owns you" (p. 154). And so, the journey was joined. In reading, I found a kindred soul in Hollis. It was as if he already knew my life, my struggles, my questions. His words and wisdom spoke deeply to me. He challenged me to find the courage not to run away from my pain but rather to lean into it and learn from it. I did not need to numb it or find distractions. He was pointing the way, but not to his path. He was pointing the way to mine. He was someone who understood the deep truth of Rumi (2004): "The cure for pain is in the pain" (p. 205). Slowly I regained my footing.

Over the years, I read Hollis's other earlier books, and waited eagerly for the new. I read, underlined, made notes in the margins, and copied sentences and paragraphs into Word documents, saved them on my computer, and printed them out for my files. I attended several of Hollis's presentations, and somehow even found enough bravery to ask him to autograph a few books. He made Jungian concepts understandable and pointed me to important passages in Jung's *Collected Works* and in his autobiography, *Memories, Dreams, Reflections*. I also reveled in Hollis's use of poetry and literature. The poems he quoted from Rilke, Dunn, and Yeats, for instance, to illustrate different themes invited me to look even deeper. The poetry added a complexity and layering to the journey. They slowed me down and asked me to ponder for a little while longer. Reading Hollis is like undertaking an archaeological dig. There is treasure waiting to be found.

I added many of Hollis's books to our departmental library at the hospital. I sent quotes to my colleagues and often dropped Hollis's name in conversations. I wanted to introduce them to this excellent resource. I made use of his metaphors and symbols in my supervision of students. I continued to review my notes and excerpts. It was a rich time; it was fun.

When I retired, my project was to go back and re-read all of Hollis's books, in order of publication, from *The Middle Passage* to *Prisms*. As I read and looked over my notes, I began to see themes emerge from one book to another. For instance, he wrote about complexes in almost all his books. It was the same concept but articulated and nuanced differently each time. Each iteration brought a deepening understanding. It was the same with other Jungian concepts. I also found he wrote about many of the primary themes of our journey: death and loss, children and parenting, religion and spirituality, and vocation, for example. I began to select and compile excerpts from my notes into different categories. The result is this book.

One of the things I learned from Hollis is that we are all asked to take risks, to live large, and to trust our soul. As Meade (2012) says, "If we fail to live out the portion of eternity given to us, no one will ever live it" (p. 107). I felt compelled to follow a poem I had written a little while earlier called "Translating Rilke,"

Rilke said:
You must change your life.

This is what he meant:
You must become
who you are meant to be—

or else die
a thousand deaths
each day.

I did not want to die another thousand deaths so I took a chance and emailed Hollis, asking for his support—his blessing, if you will—for my project. I am humbled he thought this project was worthwhile. He has been kind and generous throughout. I count him as a far-away friend but always close. I am also thankful he directed me to Chiron Publications. My thanks go to Steve Buser, Leonard Cruz, and Jennifer Fitzgerald for their encouragement and assistance. I also thank the publishers of Hollis's books for granting permission to use these selections.

This book can be read in any order by the reader. One can start with the section on Anima/Animus and read straight through to Vocation, or one can select a section and settle in there for all or some of the excerpts. The choice is to be made.

Finally, this book is dedicated to my wife, Kelli. She is the light and love of my life, my sweet companion on our journey together. I live with gratitude every day. The gods have surely smiled upon me.

Logan Jones
Raleigh, N.C.

Preface

When Logan Jones wrote to me many months ago proposing this anthology of quotes. My first thought was, "why would anybody want that book?" I think I said so at the time. My second thought was, "this will never happen." People send proposals all the time and then don't carry through. But then, just a short while back, I got the news from Logan that he had been laboring in the vineyards of all those books and done exactly what he said he was going to do. Knowing that he is a fine writer himself, I am now further in awe of his discipline, his commitment, and his scholarly mind that worked so hard on this compilation of quotes, categories, and thoughtful arrangement of topics. It must have been a labor of love, and something done in the name of love must be honored, as I do, even if I still question Logan's sanity, and the editors of Chiron for publishing this book.

Of the citations themselves, I can only say that, lifted out of context, they might at times seem arbitrary, even simplistic. I hope they stir the reader to read the original book and see where that citation fit in a larger setting. Still, it is my hope that readers will find this great work of devotion helpful to them as a source to track down a particular idea, as a moment of recognition if in their first reading, and even as a daybook of sorts to which one can turn for occasional reflection and personal application.

Perhaps it might be of some interest to the reader to talk about the writing process itself. So many folks have said to me, "writing must be so easy for you," and I wonder in return why anyone would think that. As the novelist Thomas Mann once observed, "writing is an act that is especially difficult for those who write." So it is for me, too. As a child, I had an interest in writing, and thought I might write a novel someday. That never happened. And, when I left high school, confused as most eighteen year olds are, I thought I might become a journalist. I was the Editor of the weekly campus newspaper and remember still in that ancient time, learning to set up a line of type in the "stick," an instrument printers used to hold the metal type freshly minted from the linotype machine. The type was still hot, having just been stamped from a molten alloy. Setting it in backwards was a trick, then learning to place it in the bed of the paper frame, and always discovering that metal doesn't bend to fit the columns; moreover, if the story is too long, you cut it on the spot, and too short, you make up plausible stuff to finish it. Just as having been treated with ether before surgery never leaves one's archaic memory, so the smell of burnt metal, singed wood, and the aura of ink and newsprint still warms my old soul in an era where everything now flows out of a computer into another machine somewhere else.

After I left graduate school with a doctorate in my twenties, I dutifully proved, as academia requires, that I could publish. It was an introduction to America of this new playwright named Harold Pinter whose work at that time had basically only been seen in London and New York City. The book *Harold Pinter: The Poetics of Silence* was more an exercise to demonstrate to academia than a passion, but later his oeuvre led him to the Nobel Prize, no thanks of course to my introduction. Then I dried up for over two generations. The reasons were partly that I was helping raise a family and was busy teaching, partly because of a mid-life depression, and partly because I traveled to Zürich and undertook a complete change of professional identity. While I continued to work for several years in academia, which paid the bills, increasingly my spirit was engaged with the conversation that occurs in analysis and not in the groves of Academe. When, after finishing her education, my daughter Taryn came through town and began driving across the country to her new position in a strange land called Dallas, I experienced a whiff of depression known to so many—the "empty nest" syndrome. While she was still driving across the country I asked myself that old therapist's question: "What would you tell a client who came to you with the same issues?" My response was immediate: "you have done your job here for she is the proof—she is on her own and beginning her quite separate journey. Now....now, that energy has come back to you, and what are *you* going to do with it?" I sat down that night and started writing *The Middle Passage*, a book that was my effort to make more sense of what my many, disparate clients were experiencing while asking the question: "what pattern links them together? What, for all their differences, is common to each?" All of the books, but for *The Archetypal Imagination*, which was commissioned, began this way—as a question I was asking myself. One thing I learned then, and still encounter: we do not know what we know, until we are forced to bring it into consciousness in such process as writing requires of us. So, all of them began as open questions to myself, and wound up slowly transforming into platforms for public enquiry. In between are various personal moments of indecision and uncertainty, occasional Angst, much ambiguity, and sometimes the rich moment of insight that rises from somewhere and gets transmuted to the page. It is a mysterious, alchemical process, and I am just as surprised at what sometimes emerges as the reader might be.

When I began, all of my books were haunted by the ghosts of academia, for I found myself wondering what critical voices were looking over my shoulder and critiquing everything spoken, as so commonly happens in the ivory towers. Through the years that haunting has mostly disappeared as I realized that my real audience is the reflective portion of the general public, and my mission is to be a vehicle for the immense gift and complexity of Jungian thought. To help folks understand his gift to all of us still motivates me these decades later. The one vocation that runs through all my life is teaching, and I learned that a book is simply a wall-less classroom with unknown students who are waiting for some of these ideas to help them make sense of their lives. It has been humbling to hear from many of them from distant lands and to know that the teaching matters to them.

It has often been assumed that I was gifted by grants, or free time from institutions, to produce these books. Such was never the case. Every one of them was written at night, after dinner, after a long day at work as a therapist, or administrator, with an hour here and an hour there. Put enough single hours together, and a book may result. Did I want to write at those late hours, exhausted and desirous of distraction? Of course not. Did something wish expression through me? Apparently so. Apparently a *Daimon* of some sort. On my computer I have a quote from the artist Chuck Close who said, "Inspiration is for amateurs. The rest of us just show up, and get to work." I tried to show up, over-throw doubt and lethargy, and risk it. Now, Logan Jones, himself a gifted teacher of long standing, has shown up, done his work, and I hope his assiduous labors will prove helpful to the same folks to whom I have been writing all these years.

James Hollis
Washington, D.C.

Chapter 1

Anima/Animus

Anima (Latin, "soul") The unconscious, feminine side of a man's personality. She is personified in dreams by images of females ranging from child to seductress to spiritual guide. A man's anima development is reflected in how he relates to women.

~ *The Eden Project*, p. 145

Animus (Latin, "spirit") The unconscious, masculine side of a woman's personality. The animus is personified in women's dreams by images ranging from muscle-men to poets to spiritual leaders. A woman's animus development is reflected in how she relates to men.

~ *The Eden Project*, p. 145

. . . the anima represents a man's internalized experience of the feminine, influenced by his mother and other women, and also colored by something unknown and unique to him. His experience of his anima represents his relationship to how his own body, his instincts, his feeling life and his capacity for relationship with others.

~ *The Middle Passage*, p. 46

13

The anima is the carrier of the male's relational capacity—his relationship to the body, to feeling life, to spirit, and finally to the outer woman. Whatever anima energies are not available to consciousness will invariably suffer repression, be siphoned off into the anarchic venues of the body, or go outward through projection or compulsive behaviors. The anima split that most men carry no doubt occasions their higher rate of suicide, alcoholism, and much earlier death than women, but the greatest wound of all is their estrangement from themselves, and from each other.

~ *Why Good People Do Bad Things*, pp. 44-45

The *anima,* a Latin word for *soul,* is a metaphor for man's inner life, his relationship to his body, to instinct, to feelings, to values, to spiritual aspiration. Split off from his own anima, a man will suffer depression, anger, homelessness, and proclivity to seek "her" in the outer world. The more he looks outside himself, the more he will suffer her absence.

~ *What Matters Most*, p. 50

If the anima for men represents the life-sustaining soul, the animus for women represents her spirited energy for achieving life on her own terms. When the woman's inner animus is supportive, "he" legitimizes her desires and helps her achieve them. When the animus is negative, "he" undermines her confidence, impugns her worth, and divides her energy in doubt, desuetude, deflection of eros, and depression.

~ *What Matters Most*, p. 51

Chapter 2

Archetypes

Archetypes. Irrepresentable in themselves, archetypes appear in consciousness as images and ideas, universal patterns or motifs present in the collective unconscious. Archetypal images are the basic content of religion, mythology, and art.

~ *The Eden Project*, p. 145

There is no meaning to life unless one is in touch with its archetypal roots.

~ *Tracking the Gods*, p. 63

One of the reasons we revere discoverers, explorers, and pioneers in the physical world, and those who push back the limits of mind or aesthetic expression, is because they carry for us the archetype of the hero, that complex of energy in all of us that naturally seeks to pose itself against the regressive powers of fear and lethargy in the service of individuation. When an outer hero exemplifies such action, we find a resonant energy within ourselves to similarly push back the limitations of the known. This is what Nietzsche meant by crossing the abyss on the tightrope of ourselves. The energy is there, the task is to risk walking further out into space. In that space is more freedom, a greater amplitude of soul; it is where we are meant to be.

~ *Swamplands of the Soul*, p. 139

Behind the search for the Magical Other lies the archetypal power of the parental imagos. . . . The paradigms for self, for Other, and the transactions between, are formed from these earliest experiences.

~ *The Eden Project*, p. 37

. . . the archetypal function (remember archetype as verb) does both. [That is, does the archetype originate in the human psyche alone or does it have a function transcendent to individual experience?] It is the means by which the individual brings pattern and process to chaos, and it is the means by which the individual participates in the energies of the cosmos of which we are always a part.

~ *The Archetypal Imagination*, p. 7

When a child appears in a dream, it may well betoken a possibility that already exists within the psyche but is denied or simply unconscious. This notion of the importance of the child archetype suggests that the germ of wholeness lies already within the psyche, and just as the literal child is driven by a genetic developmental plan, so the psyche unfolds the whole person through these intimations of the futurity of the child.

~ *Mythologems*, p. 40

Thus, the father imago is, as are all archetypal energies, double edged. It empowers and/or castrates; it authorizes and/or tyrannizes; it protects and/or crushes. Whenever we are dealing with our own capacity or impotence, whenever we are serving the *imago Dei* or questioning its relevance to our actual life, we are dealing with the father archetype in all its many forms.

~ *Mythologems*, p. 48

The archetype of mother is both the source of life and source of death. She is home, and sometimes, even journey, whenever we are courageous enough to accept that our journey is our home.

~ *Mythologems*, p. 48

The archetypes that arise from the deep ravines of the human psyche are not contents; they are fundamental, patterning energies.

~ *Living Between Worlds*, p. 33

Chapter 3

Children and Parents

Jung observed that the largest burden a child must bear is the unlived life of the parents.

~ *The Middle Passage*, p. 29

If we truly love our children, the single best thing we can do for them is to individuate as much as possible ourselves, for this frees them to do the same.

~ *The Middle Passage*, p. 65

As children we suffer the wounds of too-muchness or not-enoughness, feeling overwhelmed or abandoned, and wind up adapting our souls to protect our wounds. What a difference it would make in the life of child, and of the whole world, if the parent could repeatedly, sincerely, say: "You are brought into life by nature having all you need. You have a great force, a great spirit, a great energy within. Trust it, stay in contact with it, and it will always lead you towards what is right for you. Never hurt another person, but always be true to that great inner force and you will never be alone and never without direction."

~ *Tracking the Gods*, p. 131

One may see that the task of parenting is comprised of the early necessity of reassurance, and the softening of the existential blow of separation we call birth, and then the progressive abandonment of the child, in stages he or she can handle, in order to leave home at the appropriate time as a proto-adult.

~ *Creating a Life*, p. 38

The hole left by inadequate parental mirroring may only be healed by a leap of faith toward the resources within oneself.

~ *Creating a Life*, p. 106

. . . our psychologies and our theologies are profoundly colored by the imprint of our primal relationships. Those who experience the world as insufficiently there for them will have a greater need for closure, for reassurance from friends and loved ones, thus will often go out of their way to make relationship happen, for good or ill. Those who experienced the primal relationships as flooding their boundaries are more likely to avoid intimacy, maintain space in relationships, hedge on commitment or be highly selective in their friendships. Each floods the relational field with the dynamics of long ago and far away.

~ *Creating a Life*, p. 134

By whose authority do we live our lives, make our decisions, practice our professions, conduct our journeys? . . . No child can ever wholly evolve into his or her own truth with finding an authentic inner authority. For this reason, the individuation process obliges some form of overthrow of the external authority, whether modeled by the personal parent, the broader culture, or the resident tribal deity. Much sentimentalization of the family and of tradition overlooks the fact that individuation obliges some revolution, some transcendence of external authority to come to one's internal authority.

~ *Mythologems*, p. 47

These revolts against authority are the only way in which a new authority may be found. It begins with a child learning to keep something secret, to protect some part of the psyche which needs security and solitude in order to live. It takes form in the many experiments of the child, in the revolt of adolescence, in the need to move out of the house. And when these separations are not achieved, the vitality of the personality is sapped, the life which is meant to flourish withers. No matter what security is offered by staying on the home range, within the protection of a perceived authority, the gift of the developed person to the world is denied through this failure of individuation.

~ *Mythologems*, p. 47

The angst-driven search for external authority through fundamentalism is a flight from personal growth and development, an abdication of the summons to individual life.

~ *Mythologems*, p. 48

Each of us has a so-called masculine task, and each of us has a so-called feminine task. . . Our summons is both *to be* and *to do*; it is to nurture and to define; it is to be at home and journey.

~ *Mythologems*, p. 56

The first category of inevitable existential, childhood wounding we may call *overwhelment*, namely, the experience of our essential powerlessness in the face of our environment.

~ *Finding Meaning in the Second Half of Life*, p. 49

[There are three major categories of reflexive response to the existential wound of overwhelment.] First . . . *retreating, avoiding, procrastination, hiding out, denying, dissociating.* Who has not avoided what seemed painful or over-whelming? Who has not forgotten, postponed, dissociated, repressed, or simply fled? We all have. . . second . . .is in our efforts to *seize control.* . . Thirdly . . . *Accommodation* is a learned response.

~ *Finding Meaning in the Second Half of Life*, pp. 50-52

The wound of *insufficiency* tells us that we cannot rely upon the world to meet our needs.

~ *Finding Meaning in the Second Half of Life*, p. 54

[We have three major categories of response to protect our fragile psyche];. . . first. . . *to hide out from life, diminish personal possibilities, avoid risk, and even make self-sabotaging choices.* Second . . . to *overcompensate.* Third . . .

is embodied in *the anxious, obsessive need to seek the reassurance of others.*

~ *Finding Meaning in the Second Half of Life*, pp. 54-59

. . . when our child leaves—the famous empty nest syndrome—we need to say: "Job well done." Children are supposed to leave; if they don't, it would mean you had failed to empower them, ask enough of them to develop the wherewithal to conduct their lives without you. We may miss them, but if we cling to them we are not loving them; we are revealing our own dependencies. To love them is to empower them to live without us, as surely they will be obliged to in any case.

~ *Finding Meaning in the Second Half of Life*, p. 73

What would happen to our lives, our world, if the parent could unconditionally affirm the child saying in so many words: "You are precious to us; you will always have our love and support; you are here to be who you are; never try to hurt another, but never stop trying to become yourself as fully as you can; when you fall and fail, you are still loved by us and welcomed to us, but you are also here to leave us, and to go onward toward your own destiny without having to worry about pleasing us."

~ *Finding Meaning in the Second Half of Life*, p. 132

As Jung once claimed, in words which properly should haunt all parents, the greatest burden the child must bear is the unlived life of the parents . . .

~ *Finding Meaning in the Second Half of Life*, p. 133

My advice to parents is always the same: Hold your breath—they will finally grow and leave, no doubt blaming you for everything until they find that their problems have followed them. Try to model the fuller life, and such ethical standards as you wish to affirm; give permission to them to be different, to be, that is, who they are; manifest unconditional love while maintaining standards, boundaries, and reasonable expectations.

~ *Finding Meaning in the Second Half of Life*, p. 134

So the child "reads" the world: the nuances, the intimations, and internalizes the direct and indirect "instructions." So the child "interprets" the world . . . So a preoccupied parent is interpreted as he or she who will not, does not, now or ever, value me as I am, and so I must slink off into the corners of the stage, or twist myself into feats that, attention-getting at last, cause them to regard me with approval.

~ *What Matters Most*, p. 5

. . . Jung observed that the greatest burden the child must bear is the unlived life of the parent. That is, wherever the parent is stuck the child will be similarly stuck and will spend his or her life seeking to overthrow such noxious stuckness, evolving an unconscious treatment plan whose purpose is to assuage the pain of the psychic burden of this static past.

~ *Hauntings*, p. 5

. . . each child internalizes a Weltanschauung of self and the world and a set of reflexive adaptive stratagems whose purpose is to manage and to get one's needs met as well as possible in a limited universe.

~ Hauntings, p. 31

With all our blunders, the mess we make of things, the most positive influence can be the authentic life the parent provides the child. This message opens up her imagination gives her permission, and frees her to make decisions as well.

~ Hauntings, p. 34

Families are healthiest when they serve as launching pads for each person en route to his or her separate journey; they are most pathogenic when this project is subverted by its most narcissistically needy members or by the collective timidity of others to grow up, show up, and strike off on their own separate journeys.

~ Hauntings, p. 124

How different the world would be if each parent could say to the child: "Who you are is terrific, all you are meant to be. And who you *are*, as you are, is loved by all of us. You have a source within, which is called the *soul*, and it will express itself to you through what we call *desire*. Always respect the well-being of the other, but live your own journey, serve that desire, risk being that which wishes to enter the world through you, and you will always have our love, even if your path takes you away from us."

~ Hauntings, p. 129

The one thing parents can do for their children is live their lives as fully as they can, for this will open the children's imagination, grant permission to them to have their own journey, and open the doors of possibility for them. Wherever we are stuck, they will have a tendency to be stuck or will spend their life trying to overcompensate. Living our own journey as fully as possible is not only a gift to our soul, it also frees up the generation behind us to live theirs as well. The very freedom to live our lives that we wished from our parents, we thereby grant to our children to live theirs.

~ *Living an Examined Life*, p. 32

Once in a while, one finds a person whose parents, or other formative influences, granted permission, but it is very rare and, of course, requires the fortuity of a supportive cultural setting as well. Permission is something that can be given if the parents not only affirm the child in his or her struggles, but also, even more importantly, live rich, full lives themselves.

~ *Living an Examined Life*, p. 79

Perhaps the key measure of successful parenting, despite whatever mistakes we have made, is whether our children really understand that we love them as they are, not as we wish them to be.

~ *Living an Examined Life*, p. 87

. . . how can we grasp our possibilities, live our own authentic lives, if we do not model and grant overt permission for our children to live the separate journeys sought by their destiny?

~ *Living an Examined Life*, p. 88

26

. . . just imagine parents healthy enough, wise enough, mature enough, evolved enough to say to their growing children something like the following: "Who you are is terrific. You are here to become yourself as fully as you can. Always weigh the costs and consequences of your choices as they affect others, but you are here to live your journey, not someone else's and certainly not mine. I am living my journey so you won't have to worry about me. You have within you a powerful source—call it your instinct, your intuition, your gut wisdom—which will always tell you what is right for you. Serve that, respect that. Be generous to yourself and others, but always live what is right for you. Life is really rather simple: if you do what is right for you, it is right for you and others. If you do what is wrong for you, it will be wrong for you and others. Know that we may not always agree on things, and that is fine, because we are different people, not clones. Always know that I will respect you and value you no matter your choices, and you will always find here people who love you and care for you."

~ *Living an Examined Life*, pp. 89-90

And if we really do love our children, as we profess, then we have to free them of our expectations that they live like us.

~ *Living an Examined Life*, p. 90

Where I am stuck, my children will be stuck or will be diverting a significant amount of energy to compensate to get unstuck. Where I am bound by fear, by lack of permission, they will be bound. Where I am looking to others to help me evade growing up, either they will replicate my immaturity or become unduly burdened by responsibilities. As parents, mentors, leaders of one kind or another, we are called to grow up, take care of business, gain our own authentic journeys, and thus lift this terrible distraction to the soul off those whom fate has brought into our care. That is how we are healed, our children healed, and their possibilities liberated.

~ *Living an Examined Life*, p. 90

. . . wherever we are blocked, oppressed, lacking permission, so our children will be similarly blocked, will struggle in an overcompensated way to break free from our heritage, or will unconsciously evolve a "treatment plan," ranging from anaesthetizing the conflict, to distracting oneself from it, or trying to solve it. In any case, they are still carrying the haunted burden of the disowned past.

~ *Prisms*, p. 132

Chapter 4

Complexes

Complex. An emotionally charged group of ideas or images. At the core of a complex is an archetype or archetypal image.

~ *The Eden Project*, p. 145

A complex is in itself neutral, though it carries an emotional charge associated with an experiential, internalized image. The greater the intensity of the initial experience, or the longer it was reiterated, the more power the complex has in one's life. Complexes are unavoidable, because one has a personal history. The problem is not that we have complexes but that complexes have us. Some complexes are useful in protecting the human organism, but others interfere with choice and may even dominate a person's life.

~ *The Middle Passage*, p. 13

Complexes are always more or less unconscious; they are charged with energy and operate autonomously. Although usually activated by an event in the present, the psyche operates analogously, saying in effect, "When have I been here before?" The current stimulus may be only remotely similar to something that happened in the past, but if the situation is emotionally analogous then the historically occasioned response is triggered.

~ The Middle Passage, p. 13

Of all the complexes, the most influential are those internalized experiences of parents we call the mother complex and the father complex.

~ The Middle Passage, p. 13

So we all live out, unconsciously, reflexes assembled from the past.

~ The Middle Passage, p. 14

It [complex] represents an emotionally charged cluster of energy within the psyche which is partially split off from the ego and therefore can operate autonomously. It is essentially an emotional reflex whose strength depends upon the power or duration of its genesis. Some complexes are positive, though we tend to focus on those which have a negative, interruptive influence in life.

~ The Middle Passage, p. 66

A complex is an emotionally charged cluster of energy in the psyche. We may or may not be aware of such psychic charges, but when activated they have the power to temporarily take over the conscious personality.

~ Under Saturn's Shadow, p. 23

The past is not truly past. Mother and father live within, every moment—not only the personal parents, but the collective experience of them as well. Thus, feeling all the old need, the old fear, the old longing, the old anger, albeit unconsciously, men project these dynamics onto the other.

~ *Under Saturn's Shadow*, p. 111

In effect, the mother and father complexes are charged clusters of energy having a life of their own beyond the control of consciousness. Each man must inventory his own internalized imagos and discern what their message is regarding the capacity of life to sustain itself and the power to fight for still greater life. How are those clusters charged? With what messages, implicit and explicit? Where have they led to false choices?

~ *Under Saturn's Shadow*, p. 126

What we call a complex is a splinter mythology, an emotionally charged image, an implicit thought or motif, a fragmented world view that binds us to the norms of an earlier experience. The psyche is forever asking the implicit question, "When have I been here before?" The stimulation of the complex activates the historic scenario and contaminates the reality of the present.

~ *Tracking the Gods*, p. 134

As we are assemblage of behaviors, attitudes toward self and others, and charged, reflexive mythologems whose motive and contents are fueled from the past, so we find it difficult to live in the present. The more these charged imagos are

31

unconscious, the stronger the compulsion to analogously repeat the past. The ancients intuited this secret relationship and observed how fate wounds, but the responsibility for one's choices, and therefore the meaning of one's life, is still one's personal burden.

~ *Tracking the Gods*, p. 136

The signs of an activated complex . . . are that the amount of energy generated is in excess of the reasonable requirement of the situation, and that one experiences a somatic invasion, a feeling state in the body. These are clues that one is in fact experiencing a movement of psyche beneath the level of consciousness.

~ *Swamplands of the Soul*, p. 28

In time Jung speculated that there were clusters of split-off energy in us all, and these clusters he called *complexes*.

~ *Swamplands of the Soul*, pp. 117-118

A complex as such is merely an energized structure. The valency of such charged energy may be positive, negative or mixed, depending on its impact in our life. Complexes are generated by our history. We cannot avoid them because we are never free of our history. In fact, it seems that everything that has ever happened to us is still alive somewhere in the depths of our psyche. The more primal the experience, the more powerful the complex.

~ *Swamplands, of the Soul*, p. 118

Normally we do not know we are acting out of a complex because when one is activated it has the power to take over consciousness.

~ *Swamplands of the Soul*, p. 118

There are three levels of psychic reality . . . the conscious life or outer world, the personal unconscious, which is the sum of the emotional history of the individual, and the archetypal ground or collective unconscious, which is where we share common traits, drives and patterns with all humanity, past and present.

~ *Swamplands of the Soul*, p. 118

Charged personal complexes resonate throughout the psyche and activate primal emotions we have never been able to assimilate.

~ *Swamplands of the Soul*, p. 120

The activation of negatively charged complexes, and their resonance into the precarious reaches of nature, are always attended by anxiety and angst, whether we are conscious of this or not. Anxiety and angst are discomforting, unacceptable; we reflexively engage in some form of behavior to palliate our discomfort.

~ *Swamplands of the Soul*, p. 121

Since we pride ourselves on our consciousness and maturity, it is deeply disturbing to think how much of our lives is driven autonomously by our history-based patterns, buried so deeply that we may never know of their existence or silent control.

~ *Swamplands of the Soul*, p. 121

Each complex, as we have seen, has a splinter Weltan-schauung. When we are in the complex—that is, when the energic cluster has been activated and possesses us—we are in that Weltanschauung, a world-view always derived from the past, always limited to original traumatic encounters, and always forcing us to see the world through the limited imaginal lens.

~ *Swamplands of the Soul*, p. 126

. . . wherever we travel, we find our complexes, for they always travel with us.

~ *Swamplands of the Soul*, p. 129

We have wounds, and clusters of energy that accompany them, because we have a life history. The deeper question is whether we have the wounds or they have us. Such complexes, especially the parental imagos, are affectively charged images that have a unique, historically generated and discrete energy. When activated, they have the power to usurp the ego position and totally alter one's sense of reality. The parental complexes are usually the most influential because they constitute the original experience of relationship, and remain its chief paradigm. Again, because of the subjective misreading of these primal relationships, the power of the parental complexes to determine the character of subsequent relationships cannot be overstated.

~ *The Eden Project*, p. 21

The power of a complex cannot be overemphasized; indeed, it is what drives both individual history and collective culture. In particular, two great ideas, or complexes, animate the lives of us all. Both are false, and we consciously know them to be so, but we find infinite ways to deny, dissimulate, rationalize. The first great false idea is the fantasy of immortality . . . there is a place in each of us that is quick to consider ourselves exempt. Surely, we are the exceptions, somehow, and will live forever. . . The other great false idea that drives humankind is the fantasy of the Magical Other, the notion that there is one person out there who is right for us, will make our lives work, a soul-mate who will repair the ravages of our personal history; one who will be there for us, who will read our minds, know what we want and meet those deepest needs; a good parent who will protect us from suffering and, if we are lucky, spare us the perilous journey of individuation.

~ *The Eden Project*, pp. 36-37

We are reminded by ancient counsel that we should be aware of getting what we want. Depth psychology echoes this: we could be getting simply what the complex wants, what the unconscious history wants, what the unlived life wants.

~ *The Eden Project*, p. 42

When our affective response is intense and our rationalizations plentiful, we can be sure that complexes are at work. Being in an intimate relationship is a bit like asking someone to join hands with us, but only after walking across a field in which we have planted mines.

~ *The Eden Project*, p. 76

All relationships are contaminated by unconscious material, especially so when complexes have been activated. Intimate relationships naturally evoke our primal complexes because intimacy comes closest to the analogue with the original parental relationships. . . Mostly commonly activated in organizations are the parental and authority complexes.

~ *The Eden Project*, p. 105

The word *complex* . . . means the internalization of a powerful experience which, affectively charged, has the capacity to act autonomously when activated and, given its origin, in the past, tends to create repetitions—patterns based on the dynamic of its origin. . . most of the time, we are in history, for history is dynamically within us.

~ *Archetypal Imagination*, pp. 41-42

Whatsoever is unaddressed by one generation is rolled over into the next by way of example, admonition or omission. These unconscious, clustered energies, called complexes by Jung, are conveyed by direct experience internalized, or by transmission of unconscious motifs whose influence may not be seen, if at all, many years later, and often after great suffering.

~ Creating a Life, pp. 12-13

A complex is an emotionally charged, internalized experience. As life brings us large experience, from pleasant to traumatic, so such experiences are internalized as partial mythologies, provisional identities, splinter personalities. As creatures of history, we are forever imposing that history on the present moment. The earliest experiences, our primal encounters with others, most notably mother and father, constitute what one may call core complexes, for they lie at the core of who we think we are, how we experience ourselves in the world, and what we expect of it.

~ Creating a Life, p. 20

A significant part of the dilemma of our lives arises from the extent to which we are owned by the core complexes. . . When consciousness is dominated by the materials of the unconscious, one is, for all practical purposes, in the past and not in the present.

~ Creating a Life, p. 20

What is urgent in our lives? What owns us? What do we seek to transcend? These are the core complexes we serve and which govern our lives. They make the goal of creating a life very problematic indeed.

~ Creating a Life, p. 26

. . . wherever rationalizations are found, there complexes are present.

~ *Creating a Life*, p. 60

These [complexes] are energy clusters which have a life of their own, and when unchallenged, put one's life on automatic pilot.

~ *On This Journey We Call Our Life*, p. 15

A complex is a mythological subsystem that is the result of the accretion of personal experience around a certain idea. We have complexes because we have a history. . . When Jung called them feeling-toned responses to life, he was emphasizing that each core idea is charged with affect. And such affect is itself the embodiment of an idea that the psyche has provisionally formed around the experience.

~ *On This Journey We Call Our Life*, p. 26

As an image of experience, a complex is a translation, an embodiment of the invisible.

~ *On This Journey We Call Our Life*, p. 27

. . . simply being aware of a complex does not render it harmless, for the affective charge it bears continues to discharge long after initial recognition.

~ *On This Journey We Call Our Life*, p. 27

When the values are derived from an historically charged experience—and when are they not?—then we are potentially in the grip of past choices. Those choices were often dictated by surrounding circumstances; thus their values are of another time and place, often from moments less empowering and less conscious, not from this moment with its larger set of options.

~ *On This Journey We Call Our Life*, p. 28

In the Jungian approach to therapy, the task is not the elimination of complexes, as if that were possible, but redemption by honoring their power and autonomy.

~ *On This Journey We Call Our Life*, p. 29

When we ask where we are most stuck in our lives, no doubt a large moral agenda will surface. . . . We are stuck because beneath the surfaces of any issue is a set of filaments which invisibly lead back to an earlier place.

~ *On This Journey We Call Our Life*, p. 29

Wheresoever patterns are found, there are complexes at work. Wheresoever complexes are found, history prevails over the present. Wheresoever history prevails over the present, we are stuck. Wheresoever we are stuck, there is a moral task. Wheresoever there is a moral task, we will be obliged to take on some quantum of anxiety. Wheresoever we are willing to take on anxiety, we will grow and create new patterns, new history. Wheresoever we choose newly in the present, we render our journey more conscious, larger, and most possibly more consistent with what destiny demands.

~ *On This Journey We Call Our Life*, p. 31

Our stories go deep, very deep into the archetypal realm, into the genetic code, the tribal history, the family of origin, both known and repressed, as well as the mythologies we live out on a daily basis—the complexes. Each complex is a fractal of a whole world view, a value system and a sequence of programmed somatic and affective responses.

~ *Mythologems*, p. 112

When we are in the grip of a complex we are always in the past, the place of origin, and in the warp and weft of values systems of which we are only dimly aware, if at all.

~ *Mythologems*, p. 112

A complex is a cluster of energy in the unconscious, charged by historic events, reinforced through repetition, embodying a fragment of our personality, and generating a programmed response and an implicit set of expectations. . . We all have complexes because we are all historically programmed beings. Some of these programmed, reflexive responses can be helpful, as they defend us and preserve our psychological territory.

~ *Finding Meaning in the Second Half of Life*, p. 91

The energy expended through a complex always proves excessive, although the person who is possessed by the complex usually feels that the energy generated is appropriate to the situation.

~ *Finding Meaning in the Second Half of Life*, p. 93

A complex takes place when an unconscious stimulus is received.

~ *Finding Meaning in the Second Half of Life*, p. 93

When a complex is activated, not only does this stimulus trigger the stored effect tied to that issue, but it also extrapolates it into the wider range of experience, especially the fields of overwhelment and abandonment we spoke of before.

~ *Finding Meaning in the Second Half of Life*, p. 95

From the autonomous activity of these core ideas, these charged perceptions of self and world, these once accurate understandings or overgeneralizations or false readings, patterns emerge. We do not consciously intend such repetitions, but for good or ill, they have a life of their own, and bind us to the narrowness of our history rather than our capacious future, the more so because we are unconscious of their presence and their power. That of which we are not aware, owns us.

~ *Finding Meaning in the Second Half of Life*, p. 95

. . . we only begin to recognize complexes and their sabotaging effect when we have suffered their consequences, or those around us have suffered, and now call us to account.

~ *Finding Meaning in the Second Half of Life*, pp. 97-98

. . . we are led to conclude that what we call *ourselves* contains many fragments, many splinter selves. Some of

41

these darker selves are *complexes*, Jung's term for how our psyche gets charged with programmed energies during our separate histories.

~ *Why Good People Do Bad Things*, p. 4

Jung's contribution of the idea of the *complex*—a splinter personality, attached to a quantum of energy, a fragment of history, and including a micro-agenda—is most helpful.

~ *Why Good People Do Bad Things*, p. 33

In any context of intimacy, the likelihood of such primal activation of complex material is a virtual guarantee. As a historic organ, our psyche metaphorically asks: "Where have I been here before, and what did that experience tell me?" For this reason, our adult relationships have a strong tendency toward repetition of early family-of-origin dynamics.

~ *Why Good People Do Bad Things*, p. 91

Our conscious lives are driven by "pictures" and their attendant "stories." Some of these are quite conscious to us—*get a job, establish a relationship, look both ways before you cross the street,* and so on. Many more are unconscious—*do not be who you are for that is not safe, choose security over honesty, relinquish your personal authority lest it isolate you from others.* All these messages, pictures, and stories are *complexes,* namely energy-charged clusters of our history. We have complexes *because* we have histories, and history has an extraordinary power to write our biographies, frame our futures, circumscribe our freedoms.

~ *What Matters Most*, pp. 17-18

Complexes can be defined here as energized "ideas" that, mobilized, mobilize us in return. They have a point of view, a quantum of energy, and a mythological "screen" through which the world is construed, and they have an attending script that fosters a repetitive response to the ever-changing circumstances of life.

~ *What Matters Most*, p. 36, footnote

A central psychological truth, then, is *it is not what we do, but rather what our action is in service to the unconscious that matters* . . . All of us are enslaved by organizing "ideas" derived from our history.

~ *What Matters Most*, p. 38

Complexes are fractal forms, charged with energies, compelling scripts, admonitions, and outcomes, which is why so much of our histories reveal patterns even though we righteously presume and proclaim our freedoms.

~ *What Matters Most*, p. 161

Timeless sagas unwind their narrative skeins in each of us: a genetic story, older than memory; an archetypal story that forms, shapes, and directs in service to adaptation and meaning; a socially constructed story, such as gender, or race, or class, by which we are so often bewitched as to grant them ontological status despite their fictive origins. And then there are the compelling complexes which are splinter stories, splinter identities, splinter scripts, splinter mythologems. We all have complexes because we all have a history.

~ *Hauntings*, p. 3

Since a complex has a quantum of energy, charged by history, it always manifests in the body, perhaps as a constriction of the throat, a flutter in the solar plexus, tightening of the muscles, and it always floods the moment with an extra charge of affect.

~ *Hauntings*, p. 41

. . . a complex has the power to usurp the ego, plunder ordinary consciousness in the moment, oblige us to look through the regressive lens of history, and therein respond to this new moment, this new situation in an old way.

~ *Hauntings*, p. 41

. . . *what do they make us do or what do they keep us from doing?* To what degree, and in what specific moments of choice, does history govern? Thus, what is the most troubling about complexes is their capacity to remove a discriminating judgment from this moment of consciousness, assert, even impose, a historic view generated from an earlier, more likely disempowered place in our history.

~ *Hauntings*, p. 41

When the energy of a complex is activated, it always manifests in the body. . . nothing occurs in the psyche that is not also in the body.

~ *Hauntings*, p. 50

Under each stuck place there is a wire, so to speak, that reaches down into the archaic field and activates a field of anxiety of which we are largely unaware but that has enough power to reinforce whatever complex has been holding the line against change.

~ *Living an Examined Life*, p. 35

... the "reading" of our life patterns tells us much about the formative stories to which our lives have been in service, brings them to consciousness, and provides an opportunity for larger, better stories to enhance our journeys. If we only change behavior and ignore its charged locus in our unconscious, the early "story" will only migrate into a new venue, a different relationship, a recurrent dilemma. These emotionally charged "stories" or "complexes" are splinter personalities, fractal scripts, and somatic presences. Until the core perception or idea that generates the undesirable behavior, the avoidance, the self-defeating compliance is identified, challenged, and worked with over time, the psyche stays stuck, the soul stagnates, and suffering persists.

~ *Living Between Worlds*, p. 25

We carry all that history with us, organized in clusters called "complexes," shards of experience that are activated by any new visitant seen from the perspective of the old frame. Some of our complexes are helpful, supportive; some are pernicious and infantilizing. But all complexes, to some degree, 1) pull us out of this moment, 2) relocate us in the time and context of its creation, and 3) link us to the understanding, the limited frame, and the constrained behavior of that time, that place, and frequently, the powerlessness of that distant hour.

~ *Prisms*, p. 31

All complexes are "stories," not the reality, but the constructs, the narratives, the fragmentary interpretations of the mysterious world around us, and not the reality itself.

~ *Prisms*, pp. 31-32

We have complexes because we have histories, and these charged shards of internalized experience, replete with bodily manifestation (a flush of nausea, sweating palms, constricted throat); a rush of energy that piles on the present moment the monstrous enormity of the past; an archaically ground lens through which the new may only be see through the perspective of the old; and an attendant script, with splinter personalities, driving the reenactment of mythologems with replicative outcomes.

~ *Prisms*, p. 94

The recognition of patterns in our lives, especially those that undermine our own legitimate self-interest, is ample testimony to the living presence of affect-laden, imaginal threads with the power to compel ego assent, provide ready rationalization to legitimize the complex, and enact the script to which that image is attached.

~ *Prisms*, p. 109

The gift of dreams, symptoms, encounters with wisdom literature, and other modes of insight and inspiration are specifically counter to the iron wheel of complex and its grim repetition.

~ *Prisms*, p. 109

Every *complex* is an embodied philosophy, rooted in the subject's past, a splinter personality, a somatic manifestation, a mini-script or scenario, and a tendency toward repetition.

~ *Prisms*, p. 135

Chapter 5

Conscious and Unconscious

Loss, grief, and betrayal are not just dismal places we must unwillingly visit, they are integral to the maturation of consciousness. They are as much a part of the journey as the places we feel respite and would tarry.

~ *Swamplands of the Soul*, p. 51

No influences are more pervasive, or determinative, than those of which one is unaware. We inherit not only the Zeitgeist of our fated time and place, but also the implicit world-view of the tribe and the family of origin.

~ *Creating a Life*, p. 71

As Jung said time and again, whoever has discovered the power of the unconscious knows thereafter that he is not the master in his own house.

~ *On This Journey We Call Our Life*, p. 25

It is the chief delusion of the ego that it knows, that it is in control, when in fact it almost blindly serves some autonomous quasi-mythological fragment. . . . Most of the time we serve whatever charged history fate has provided.

~ *On This Journey We Call Our Life*, p. 26

. . . unconscious value systems run our lives, make our choices, live their consequences, and cause the unfolding of repetitive patterns.

~ *On This Journey We Call Our Life*, p. 52

The depth of our journey will be found in this dialectical exchange with oneself. The role of the unconscious is to provide correctives or compensation that serve to enlarge a person.

~ *On This Journey We Call Our Life*, p. 89

The problem always comes back to the fact that we do not know what we do not know. We are not conscious of that of which we are unconscious. We do not apprehend that which lies beyond our instruments of apprehensions.

~ *Mythologems*, p. 29

The worst thing we can do to others is burden them with our unconscious material, and yet we cannot avoid doing so.

~ *Mythologems*, p. 126

Codependence is predicated on one's reflexive assumption of powerlessness and the inordinate power of the other. . . Learning to find one's own truth, hold to it, and negotiate with others seems easy enough on paper. In practice, it means catching reflexive actions while they occur, suffering the anxiety aroused by acting more consciously in integrity, and tolerating the assault of anxiety-driven "guilt" thereafter.

~ *Finding Meaning in the Second Half of Life*, p. 53

Almost everyone has some addictive patterns. Any reflexive response to stress and anxiety, whether conscious or not, is a form of addiction. The chief motive of any addiction is, of course, to help one feel what in fact one has already been feeling. Breaking the tyranny of addiction will require one to feel the pain that the addiction defends against. No wonder, then, that addictive patterns have such staying power as flimsy, faltering defenses against primal wounds.

~ *Finding Meaning in the Second Half of Life*, p. 61

The tyranny of the past is never greater than when we do not recall. Faulkner once opined that the past is not dead; it is not even past.

~ *Finding Meaning in the Second Half of Life*, p. 63

No freedom is possible, no authentic choice, where consciousness is lacking. Paradoxically, consciousness usually only comes from the experience of suffering and the flight from suffering is why we often elect to remain in the constrictive yet familiar old shoes. But the psyche is never silent, and suffering is the first clue that something is soliciting our attention and seeking healing.

~ *Finding Meaning in the Second Half of Life*, p. 64

The problem with the unconscious is that it is unconscious.

~ *Why Good People Do Bad Things*, p. 29

Count on the fact that *whatever we deny within, we will compulsively seek in the outer instead.* When we have not valued *Eros as the search for greater knowledge of self and*

49

world, then we are far more likely to become enslaved to our projects and projections—whether sex, substance, symbol, or relational addiction—for nothing holds greater power over us than our unconsciousness, which perforce makes decisions on our behalf throughout the conduct of daily life.

~ *What Matters Most*, p. 53

While there are conscious stories we claim as ours, unconscious stories we enact everyday prove over time even more intimately ours.

~ *What Matters Most*, p. 166

The present is haunted by the archetypal dynamics which remind us that any story untold is an unconscious present. An unconscious present is a story which will insist on being told and will spill into our biographies. Over the entrance to his home, Jung carved a phrase from Erasmus: "Bidden or unbidden, God will be there."

~ *Hauntings*, p. 13

What I have ignored, you as friend, partner, client will be obliged to deal with sooner or later, and vice versa. Just how conscious, how loving, how fair, how considerate is that? How can I not work on myself when not only I but you and others suffer my many avoidances?

~ *Hauntings*, p. 108

When I admit that the only person present at every moment in every scene of the long-running soap opera I call my life is me, then I am obliged to admit that, despite the profound ministries of fate and the choices of others, I am somehow responsible for the patterns, the replicative consequences, and the many estrangements from self and others that keep showing up in my life.

~ *Hauntings*, p. 108

The problem with the unconscious is that it is *unconscious*.

~ *Prisms*, p. 142

... the question that has to be addressed by all who wish to live consciously in the modern world is: "*By what values am I living my life, or what values are living in me, without my consent, without my understanding?*"

~ *Prisms*, pp. 174-175

Chapter 6

Death and Loss

Death is the great leveler, and there are no exceptions.

~ *The Eden Project*, p. 119

It is not so much that death shocks or surprises us . . . but that there are, finally, no exceptions, no exemptions.

~ *Archetypal Imagination*, p. 4

So Death, which accompanies the baby's cry, which stands watching at our side, and whose imperatives none can deny, requires us to become conscious, to become creatures of choice. *We have been granted mortality that we might have meaning, and have it abundantly.*

~ *Archetypal Imagination*, p. 53

This fate we have, to be mortal beings and to be conscious of that mortality, also begets our destiny, which is to bring meaning into the world, to create a life and a sensibility for which only the word *praise* may suffice.

~ *Archetypal Imagination*, p. 53

In the Western world, good health is well on its way to supplanting materialism as the new religion.

~ *On This Journey We Call Our Life*, p. 94

Certainly death as quickener is the frequent catalyst for urgency of choice.

~ On This Journey We Call Our Life, p. 96

Of course we may wish to value friends, places, experiences of the past. Carrying them with us is how we honor their worth to us. But nostalgia is also an excuse for avoiding growth, for refusing to pick up the next stage of our journey, especially the painful parts. To commit to love another is also to commit to their loss, for one will inevitably leave the other. To commit to growth means that one will have to leave safe places and venture into the unknown. But that is where the soul will enlarge.

~ On This Journey We Call Our Life, p. 99

How we approach the meaning of our journey is closely tied to how mindful we are of our mortality. Such mindfulness is not morbid; it quickens consciousness, helps us differentiate the trivial from the enduring, calls us to choice rather than vacillation, and, in the face of annihilation, relocates us in the context of compelling mystery.

~ On This Journey We Call Our Life, p. 104

Is death not our daily companion? We have all died many deaths . . . There are many ways of dying. Death is only one of them.

~ On This Journey We Call Our Life, p. 105

Though character can be formed, and modified, we all have inherent tendencies. . . Put most succinctly, having been given life, what we now owe fate is two things, a life fully lived, and our death in return. However much the nervous ego or the neurotic culture wishes otherwise, *we all owe life a death. In fact, perhaps we owe life many of them.*

~ *What Matters Most*, p. 202

The avoidance of our mortal, transient condition is pathological. To be mindful of our fragile fate each day, in a non-morbid acknowledgement, helps us remember what is important in our life and what is not, what matters, really, and what does not. It has been my experience that those who handle aging and mortality least well are those who fear that they have not been in *this* life, that they have not been *here*, that they have not lived the life they were called to live.

~ *Finding Meaning in the Second Half of Life*, p. 209

All rising things fall; all ascendant things return to earth; all bodies in motion submit to the law of inertia. The pragmatic question that confronts us, then, is *what does this fact make us do, or keep us from doing?* And how might we live more *abundantly* in the presence of our mortality? And, finally, does mortality even matter? . . . an aroused awareness of mortality is the same as fear of mortality.

~ *What Matters Most*, p. 212

Loss seems to be the price of abundance, the counterpoise to the richness of life, and remains always, even in moments of attainment, its silent, necessary companion.

~ *Finding Meaning in the Second Half of Life*, p. 215

Grief is honest acknowledgement of loss, which is based on honest acknowledgement of value. . . We cannot have the richness without the possibility of loss, and without loss we cannot fully treasure the gifts we have been given.

~ *Finding Meaning in the Second Half of Life*, p. 216

Whatever we think, feel, believe, hope, from a limited ego frame, is literally irrelevant to the mystery of mortality itself. In death, either the ego is radically transformed in ways we cannot even imagine, or it is annihilated.

~ *What Matters Most*, p. 224

There is real emotion, real cost attendant upon growth and its necessary losses, but excessive attachment is the enemy of the life force itself.

~ *What Matters Most*, p. 225

With a mature engagement with the mystery that our mortality demands, we may find that our goals change, and change significantly. We may begin to prize depth over abundance, humility over arrogance, wisdom over knowledge, growth over comfort, and meaning over peace of mind.

~ *What Matters Most*, p. 226

The question is not how to solve our mortal condition; that is hubris and delusion. The question rather is: How to live? Paradoxically, mortality, our most unwelcome guest, is a friend, for it requires that question of us, the addressing of which brings us whatever quality we can manage in this short, precious life.

~ *What Matters Most*, pp. 234-235

. . . we all have separate lives, separate journeys, separate destinies, and we do not serve those lost by abrogating or sabotaging our own summons to live. Rather, we are reminded to live even more consciously in the face of loss and to treasure what relationships, and what tasks of growth, are still around us.

~ *Hauntings*, pp. 66-67

There is no going forward without a death of some kind: a death of who we thought we were and were supposed to be; a death of a map of the world we thought worthy of our trust and investment; a death of expectations that by choosing rightly we could avoid suffering, experience the love and approval of those around us, and achieve a sense of peace, satisfaction, arrival home. But life has other plans it seems; indeed, our own souls have other plans. And there is a terrible price to pay for ignoring or fleeing those intimations and summons to depth.

~ *Living an Examined Life*, p. 61

The word *grief* comes from the Latin *gravis*, which means "heavy," from which we get *grave* and *gravity*. Grieving is a weight upon the spirit, to be sure. Yet, the way to honor grief is to experience it fully, knowing that we grieve whatever was of value to us. The way to continue our honoring is to carry that value forward and serve it as best we can.

~ *Living Between Worlds*, p. 109

Let us risk letting go of our fearful, tenuous grip on life whereby, ironically, we remain enslaved to the fear of death. Let us embrace dying unto our previous life, and the fear that keeps us from the new lest we die before we die.

~ *Prisms*, pp. 200-201

Chapter 7

Depression

A depression at midlife, or indeed at any time when the psyche wishes enlargement or transition, indicates a suppression of the life force.

~ *Swamplands of the Soul*, p. 71

Often, to lift a depression we have to risk taking on that which we fear most, that which is blocking our natural growth.

~ *Swamplands of the Soul*, p. 72

Depression is compensation in that it obliges us to pay attention to an altered reality. To "consciously regress" is to go along with the depression, to swim to the bottom of the well in order to find its treasure.

~ *On This Journey We Call Our Life*, pp. 123-124

. . . the way *through* a depression is through it and not out of it. Going through it will reveal its meaning, and unfold what the secret will of the Self may be.

~ *Mythologems*, p. 66

Avoidance of this openness to going down and through will keep one in the form of spiritual adolescence, not unlike those whose spirituality is always "up there," safe from any real engagement with life. The bouncy spirituality of the so-called New Age movement and many fundamentalist groups is not only a flight from reality, with its necessary and autonomous visitations to the swamplands of the soul, but a shunning of the hero task as well. There are monsters, there are dragons, there are dangerous depths, and they are within us all the time. They are what give us our *gravitas* and our great capacity for enlargement through holding the tension of opposites.

~ *Mythologems*, p. 66

The ancient stories are replete with descents, the catabasis to the underworld: Orpheus, Odysseus, Jesus, Aeneas, Dante, and many others. What is to be found down there? Certainly darkness, often monsters, sometimes treasures, and always something useful.

~ *Mythologems*, p. 70

The darkness down there is also the darkness of the womb, from which springs new life as well as the darkness of the tomb. Our fear of such nether places is projected onto spiders, serpents, mice, bats, and other denizens of the dark.

~ *Mythologems*, p. 71

Before one can deepen as a person, one must visit the deeps within. We cannot ascend without first descending.

~ *Mythologems*, p. 74

What is denied above will assert itself from below.

~ *Mythologems*, p. 75

One of the first signs of this descent is ennui, or boredom, perhaps even in the career for which one prepared so diligently. . . The ascent requires not only the climb out of the depths, but also the necessary task of integrating what has been learned into consciousness.

~ *Mythologems*, p. 75

The daily confrontation with these gremlins of fear and lethargy obliges us to choose between anxiety and depression, for each is aroused by the dilemma of daily choice. Anxiety will be our companion if we risk the next stage of our journey, and depression our companion if we do not.

~ *Finding Meaning in the Second Half of Life*, pp. 39-40

It takes a great deal of psychological honesty to be able to look directly at our sorrow and take responsibility for what personal task has now emerged.

~ *Finding Meaning in the Second Half of Life*, p. 73

Sometimes these depressions take us over and leave us prostrate. At the bottom of this well, and there is always a bottom, there is a clear task and a summons. The task is to ask what the psyche wants, not what the parents want, not what the parent complexes want, not what the culture wants, not what the ego wants.

~ *Finding Meaning in the Second Half of Life*, p. 75

The sense of ennui, restlessness, sometimes even depression that comes with the achievement of one's ambitions, or the failure to achieve them, is the generally unwelcome invitation to disidentify with those goals.

~ *Finding Meaning in the Second Half of* Life, p. 152

What, then, is the summons of my soul?

~ *Finding Meaning in the Second Half of Life*, p. 224

What is depression but life wishing to express itself but being "pressed down?" What wishes to live within us? Find that, and give it energy, value, and enactment in the world, and the depression will lift. So we need to ask: "Where am I stuck, blocked by archaic fears, and therefore repeating, reinforcing the conditions that have produced my disabling depression?"

~ *Finding Meaning in the Second Half of Life*, pp. 225-226

The therapeutic secret of a depression is not found by suppressing it with biochemical agents, but by asking its meaning. This investigative approach is enlarging, and the soul will not fail to offer direction if we are willing to be open.

~ *Finding Meaning in the Second Half of Life*, p. 227

Chapter 8

Ego and Self

Ego. The central complex of consciousness. A strong ego can relate objectively to activated contents of the unconscious (i.e., other complexes) rather than identifying with them.

~ *The Eden Project*, p. 145

Self. The archetype of wholeness and regulating center of the psyche, experienced as a numinous power that transcends the ego (e.g., God).

~ *The Eden Project*, p. 146

The ego, our conscious sense of who we are, is an affectively charged cluster of replicated experience. It is the central complex of consciousness whose boundaries are fluid, malleable, and easily violated. We need ego to conduct the business of conscious life, to mobilize psychic energy and direct it toward goals, to maintain a degree of self-consistency and continuity so that we can move from day to day, context to context. But the central project of the ego is security which, understandably, stands over against the surge of unconscious material from within, and encounters the massive onslaught of energies from without.

~ *Swamplands of the Soul*, pp. 11-12

... the Self is an activity of the psyche whose function is to further the development of the individual

~ *Swamplands of the Soul*, p. 12

We all live lives estranged—from others, from the gods, and worst of all from ourselves... We know that we are our own worst enemies. We never stop seeking to reconnect, to find home again, and in the end we simply leave it in a different way.

~ *The Eden Project*, p. 11

... the quality of all of our relationships is a direct function of our relationship to ourselves.

~ *The Eden Project*, p. 13

The best thing we can do for our relationships with others, and with the transcendent, then, is to render our relationship to ourselves more conscious.

~ *The Eden Project*, p. 13

The Self, like God, is essentially unknowable. So one must speak both of the mystery of God and the mystery of the Self. The Self is not an object or even a goal, but an activity, a process.

~ *The Eden Project*, p. 16

The capacity of the ego to accept ambiguity is central to emotional maturity. In fact, how we can hold what I call the triple As—ambiguity, ambivalence, and anxiety—in tension is a test of our psychic strength.

~ *Archetypal Imagination*, p. 63

. . . Jung's view of the Self as that which is essentially mysterious, unknowable, but which expresses itself autonomously and whose effects may occasionally be made conscious. . . It allows us to discern patterns, replication, consistency, which in time we differentiate through other words like character, temperament, even typology.

~ *Creating a Life*, pp. 28-29

Jung asserts the multiplicity of selves, sees the Self as *doing* not being, and thus converts Self from noun into verb *selving*.

~ *Creating a Life*, p. 31

. . .we have to learn to live with and respect the mysteries anew, knowing that our fictions are fictions. Such courage before the abyss of possibility is the only way in which the mystery can be honored.

~ *Creating a Life*, p. 32

The Self is that which directs us, ineluctably, even in the face of immense contrary pressures, towards ourselves. We may live in bad faith with the Self, but something in us knows that, and registers its protest whether we pay attention or not. Something in us pulls us towards ourselves quite apart from how the ego or the tribe would arrange things.

~ *Creating a Life*, p. 81

. . . the Self stands at the core of being. It has very little to do with what the ego or the tribe intends, rather it is the carrier of what the soul intends.

~ *Creating a Life*, p. 87

The metaphor of the Self arises from our intuitive knowledge that something within each of us not only monitors our organic, biochemical processes, develops us from less complex to more complex creatures, but, much more, seeks that state of being that is the apparent purpose of our incarnation in the first place.

~ *Finding Meaning in the Second Half of Life*, pp. 4-5

. . . the Self is in service to the soul; which is to say, the directive, purposeful energies that govern our lives are themselves in service to meaning, though a transcendent meaning that often has little to do with our narrow frame of conscious understanding.

~ *Finding Meaning in the Second Half of Life*, p. 5

The Self is the embodiment of the totality of life of the organism. It is the architect of wholeness.

~ *Finding Meaning in the Second Half of Life*, p. 10

The ego wishes comfort, security, satiety; the soul demands meaning, struggle, becoming.

~ *Finding Meaning in the Second Half of Life*, p. 71

Notice that the responsibility always comes back to us: we cannot ask of the other what we should do for ourselves.

When we do what we need to do for our own enlargement, we serve others, and achieve the moral enlargement to support their development as well. Such relationship, whether the intimate marriage, or the effective family, is in service not to the selfish agenda but to the Self, which is in turn in service to the soul. The ultimate test of the family is not whether it provides safety and predictability, but whether or to what degree each person can leave it, freely, and return, freely as a larger person.

~ *Finding Meaning in the Second Half of Life*, p. 142

In the second half of life the ego is periodically summoned to relinquish its identifications with the values of others, the values received and reinforced by the world around it. It will have to face potential loneliness in living the life that comes from within rather than according to the noisy clamor of the world, or the insistency of the old complexes. It will have to submit itself to that which is truly larger, sometimes intimidating, and always summoning us to grow up. It will need to live by verifications from within, not through acquiescence to the timidities of its times.

~ *Finding Meaning in the Second Half of Life*, p. 153

Guilt denied will find some other way through which the piper will be paid. The capacity to accept responsibility for this harm, for choices made, for choices not made marks the maturity level of the ego and gravity to the soul.

~ *Finding Meaning in the Second Half of Life*, p. 213

The human ego is itself a complex, that is, an historically charged energy system that serves as a centrum, a point of focus that provides consciousness, intentionality, consistency, and continuity—all important tools of learning, social functioning, even survival.

~ *Why Good People Do Bad Things*, p. 184

As a complex amid other complexes, the ego is easily frightened, easily nudged off its center, and learns from the earliest days that adaptation serves survival. So we learn to adapt to the demands around us, real or perceived. In time we even tend to identify with our adaptations rather than our intrinsic nature.

~ *Why Good People Do Bad Things*, p. 185

Let us recall for a moment that our ego—which seems to us our center, our core, our identity, our rock of ages—is itself one "complex" among many. It is the central complex of consciousness—*who we think we are* at any given moment, but in any given moment that "complex," malleable as it is, may be subsumed by other energies with quite contrary agendas, scripts, and provisional identities, and together they collusively produce unpredictable outcomes.

~ *What Matters Most*, p. 95

Our egos are fragile wafers on a vast sea, even as our separate biographies float in the flotsam and jetsam of histories not our own.

~ *Hauntings*, p. xvi

In every moment, the ego is driven to fixate, stop, grab hold of, and control, even while cells are dying, rebirthing, and transforming.

~ *Hauntings*, p. 2

Disconnected from it [the Self], we serve our complexes, our wounds, and received cultural and familial messages instead of serving the intent of our soul. Working with our dreams allows all of us to look within, to see the center of gravity shift from our many adaptations to the outer world to begin to trust that something within each of us knows what is right for us. Learning to trust that sorting process, to value the dialogue, and to risk relying on an internalized sense of authority is what restores our journey to us, bringing us back to our souls.

~ *Living Between Worlds*, p. 26

. . . the ultimate decisions of our lives are made by some higher agency than the ego. Ego intentionality is tasked with the governance of daily life. But when ego consciousness can accord itself with the will of the Self, there is profound sense of rightness, the peace, the accord that comes from a moment of wholeness when we are at one with ourselves, and not this split, warring, assemblage of fractious parties.

~ *Living Between Worlds*, p. 134

Whenever we are obliged to radically reframe our sense of self and world, we are in the presence of mystery.

~ *Prisms*, p. 28

Narcissus wishes to be seen, and to be seen, wholly. And valued, as he is. And so do we . . . Perhaps also the Self is that capacious power within each of us that sees and hold us with care as we tumble through an infinite space into the depths of our own fathomless mysteries.

~ *Prisms*, p. 125

Chapter 9

The Gods

A god dies when the principle it dramatizes has been forgotten or superseded. A god dies when the dynamic principle it embodies has lost its energy. A god dies when that energy departs the vessel of concept or image and goes underground or takes on a new form.

~ *Tracking the Gods*, p. 60

When consciousness neglects the shadowy parts and inflates its own importance, the gods grow interested, draw near, and bring about the restoration of balance.

~ *Tracking the Gods*, p. 69

We can, therefore, only know the gods as psychic events, for psychic events, that is, internalized experiences, are all we can ever know. Far from demanding the idea of the divine, or elevating the human, this is a simple, common-sense recognition of the limits of human cognition and verification on the one hand, and the absolute reality of the inner world on the other.

~ *Tracking the Gods*, p. 100

... trying to stuff all the positive attributes into a single god, excluding those that are contradictory or embarrassing, has created quite a shadow for most theologies.

~ *Tracking the Gods*, p. 102

In antiquity, as communities migrated, the gods often put off their former attire, donned local garments, even changed their names to the local epithets. But the principles they embodied did not change; regardless of nomenclature, the same divine, that is mythic, principles were being acknowledged. Whether her name be Hera, Juno, Isis, Sophia, or Mary, the Great Mother is present. . . . By ignoring or denying their so-called pagan sources, modern religions cut themselves off from their archetypal ground.

~ *Tracking the Gods*, p. 102

... to define a god from a mythic perspective as *something that is intimated by, and present in, the affectively charged image that emerges from an experience in depth, an arche--typal encounter.*

~ *Tracking the Gods*, pp. 102-103

... when the intellect severs the symbolic image from the affective charge, or when the institution crushes the spontaneity of the imago, then the god dies. . . Only the hidden god is the true god, for the god who can be known has already become an artifact of conscious culture and is in the process of disappearing.

~ *Tracking the Gods*, p. 104

Tracking the gods means paying feeling attention to the incarnation of the archetypal images, whether they occur in the venue of dream, somatic complaint or political event. Images that spring from the head only are, like certain progeny of Zeus, deformed; they are merely ideologies, doomed to partiality and rapid decay.

~ *Tracking the Gods*, p. 106

To ignore the gods is to guarantee that they will exact some form of revenge in the privacy of neurosis or the horrific theater of history.

~ *Tracking the Gods*, p. 107

... the gods are dynamic energies that rise out of archetypal encounters. They leave their traces in luminous images, but the images are not the gods; they are temporary containers of that divine energy. How natural it is for the human to grasp at the image in order to hold the energy, possess the god. This impulse manifests as idolatry and its wicked stepchild, ideology. Nothing drives the godly energy away faster than our desire to fix it in its evanescent course.

~ *Tracking the Gods*, p. 116

The figures that animated ancient mythology move through our souls, trouble sleep and sometimes act out in unsettling ways. The scenarios of ancient script are now visible in the plots we have been enacting, albeit in a thousand thousand variations, and we knew it not.

~ *Tracking the Gods*, p. 117

But the ancients had it right—wherever there is depth, there is also the divine. Where the gods are is where meaning may be experienced. What the gods ask most of us is that we attend them, that is, bear conscious witness to their energies, of which their forms are but the material husks.

~ *The Eden Project*, p. 34

Archetypally speaking, the god-image emerges from our own depths. A god is defined then as an affectively charged image that emerges out of our encounter with Mystery. Such images are numinous; they wink at us and activate a resonant response.

~ *The Eden Project*, p. 127

. . . we know that all things which emanate from the human bear the mark of the human, that we cannot help but anthropomorphize the unknowable. What we say about God is finally saying more about ourselves than the mystery we call God.

~ *The Eden Project*, p. 116

The internal carrier of the god-imago is what Jung called the Self.

~ *The Eden Project*, p. 122

How can a god, immortal by definition, die? What dies is rather the power of the image to point beyond itself toward the Mystery it once intimated. The idolatry of image occurs after the image has already gone elsewhere. . . Fundament-alism and literalism are in the end soul denying.

~ *The Eden Project*, p. 128

Whatever the gods and goddesses are, or whatever the psyche intends through our dreams, is surely driven from those images when we encapsulate them in concepts.

~ *Archetypal Imagination*, p. 5

Perhaps what the gods demand of us is not slavish worship, nor infantilizing imitation, or apotropaic denial, but simply to be remembered, to be respected as the truths which do not die as everything else will. To hold a candle of consciousness in the darkness, to pay homage to the power of the multigenerational influences which we carry into daily life, means that our relationships with the past might prove less troubled and our movement through the twin worlds which we inhabit might be richer.

~ *Archetypal Imagination*, p. 76

As Jung has observed, what is denied inwardly, will come to us as Fate. . . The gods set things in motion, but the choices are ours. The sum of those choices, and their consequences which may ripple through generations to come, is the story of our life.

~ *Creating a Life*, p. 35

. . . no matter how sincere our theologies, our beliefs, may be, however grounded in primal experience, the gods slip away from original creed and ritual to undermine consciousness by changing their shape, moving deeper and reappearing somewhere else in a different guise.

~ *On This Journey We Call Our Life*, p. 27

To talk of the gods is to respect the autonomy and profundity of the energies of the cosmos. As Jung has argued, it is the encounter with the numinous that is the true goal of therapy.

~ *On This Journey We Call Our Life*, p. 70

Our lives are an invitation to conscious reflection, a challenge to bear witness to a large symbolic drama which courses through history and through individuals. While the deeper intent of such intimations may puzzle, even frighten the ego, service to those great energies we call the gods obliges a more respectful relationship than that which we have more commonly lived.

~ *Mythologems*, pp. 17-18

The nature gods are much older than the gods of the head; the gods of the loins more ancient than the gods of the heart; the gods of earth and sea more ancient than gods of the skies.

~ *Mythologems*, p. 73

Anything which the finite mind presents as a construct of the infinite reveals more of human imagination than of the infinite itself. . . The god is incarnated by consciousness through the image which arises out of such encounters. The image presented to consciousness is not the god, limited as it is to the inadequate tools of finite sensibility, yet such an image is filled with, and driven by, energy which derives from the god.

~ *Mythologems*, pp. 81-82

How often the gods appear to us that way, full of mystery, full of riddles, full of paradoxes that crack the brain and divide the heart. But those are the gods for you, and that is why they are gods.

~ *Mythologems*, p. 88

The gods arise out of our encounter with depth, with mystery.

~ *Mythologems*, p. 88

When the word spread throughout the ancient world that the great nature god Pan was dead, there was no rejoicing. He was replaced by the stern monotheistic gods of the Judeo-Christian-Islamic world, who were in turn replaced by the modern reigning deities of Positivism, Materialism, Hedonism, and most of all, the great god Progress. And the world gets emptier and emptier, and the clients pile up in therapists' offices, huddle fearfully in houses of ancestral worship, or numb out through television, drugs or even an obsessive preoccupation with health. The gods have hardly gone; they have simply gone underground, and they constantly resurface in the form of our various pathologies

~ *Mythologems*, p. 89

Gods ignored, which is to say, primal energies repressed, split off, projected, today show up as neuroses. They are the animating wounds manifest in history, acted in families, public forums or the sundry deformations of the private soul.

~ *Mythologems*, p. 90

Looked at archetypally, a god is an image which arises out of a depth experience, and encounter with mystery. For this reason, divinity is always renewing itself. How could it possibly be fixed? It is energy, not image. The image is only the transient husk of divinity.

~ *Mythologems*, p. 91

So, who says the gods have gone? They have simply departed the old husks and have moved invisibly into new loci.

~ *Mythologems*, p. 97

Each of these cultural forms seeks to retain a vital connection to the primal experience, to recreate the wonder and terror of first things. But the passage of time takes one further and further from the initial wonder or terror. As a result, the ego tends to seek its former level of satisfaction and reiterates with greater urgency. So, even as one urgently, even frantically, seeks to maintain the divine aura of dogma, rigidify the ritual, and convert the cultic experience to cultic security, the gods slip away and grown invisible again. At those moments a person, a tribe, a civilization experiences a profound crisis of identity, meaning and direction. Such a dilemma is the story of our time.

~ *Mythologems*, p. 98

To ask, "what god is at work here, what god forgotten, offended, split off, projected," is to undertake the healing task of therapy. And yet this sort of metaphoric formulation is ridiculed by most representatives of the modern therapeutic community.

~ *Mythologems*, p. 98

The loss of relationship to the invisible powers makes the visible powers all the more powerful.

~ *Mythologems*, p. 99

The gods have hardly departed; they have simply gone underground and reappear as wounds, as inflations, as pathologies. Our contemporary suffering is not tragic, for we wrestle not with gods; rather it is pathetic, the suffering which is unconscious and invariably victimizing of self and others.

~ *Mythologems*, p. 99

What the gods ask of us is that we remember them, that we acknowledge their presence in every moment, even when we sleep, even when we are in motion, even when we think we are who we believe we are. To the omnipresent gods we are obliged to bring our recalcitrant soul, every day, in all its humiliations and petty triumphs, and confess, "Your student, however slow, is willing / the only student you'll ever have."

~ *Mythologems*, p. 100

For sure our sentimentality and our tendency toward anthropomorphizing desires a more personable god; that is, *someone much more like us,* having of course the same moral values we espouse, and no doubt the same tastes in interior decoration, theories on how the world should be run, etc. But we can see from the vast pantheon of deities that many are without those personal characteristics which make us feel comfortable. Quite the contrary, they often confront us in brutal, impersonal ways.

~ *Mythologems*, p. 103

... if the gods are diseases, then our diseases are religious. If the gods are personifications of the forces which run the universe, then our disorders are violations of those energies and their teleological intentions for us.

~ *Mythologems*, p. 109

The real work of therapy is to approach the numinous, to be awed again, frightened, uplifted by it as we were as children, and to experience the will of the gods at work in our bones, our dreams and, perhaps, through the enlargement of consciousness.

~ *Mythologems*, p. 111

The flight from the summons of the gods is the chief pathology of our time and all of us have fallen into it.

~ *Mythologems*, p. 117

The difficulty in transmitting original revelation leads to dogma, rites and cultic practices. Dogma grows around an experience in order to explain it, to defend it, to communicate it to others. Obviously, the dogma as such bears no mystery, though it may speak in great sincerity of that original experience of it. Rituals have as their motive the recreation and, hopefully, the reanimation of the original experience, the *participation mystique* that accompanies phenomenological experience. In time, through reiteration, rituals can grow rigid and lose their capacity to reconnect a participant to the primal affect. Similarly, cultic practice, that which differentiates one tribal experience from another, can in time see arbitrary.

~ *Mythologems*, p. 133

As a result of the slippage of affective connection to the original image, institutions grow up around such experience in an effort to sustain the treasure which animated the elders.

~ *Mythologems*, p. 133

When we take the gods as *facts,* rather than metaphors, then we get lost in debating the merits of the facts rather than appreciating their meaning.

~ *Mythologems*, p. 134

As we all know, the early history of the Bible reports divinity repeatedly chastising the faithful for reifying their divine experience, transforming the spirit into images. We are not superior to our predecessors; we are all prone to idolatry when we forget that the image is meant to point beyond itself toward the ineffable. The symbol points toward the godly, but it is not the god.

~ *Mythologems*, p. 139

"God" is a metaphor for what wholly transcends our capacity to comprehend, expressed through primal forces which we nonetheless experience.

~ *Mythologems*, p. 139

The gods want us to grow up, to step up to that high calling that each soul carries as its destiny. Choosing the path that enlarges rather than diminishes will serve us well in navigating through our idol-ridden, clamorous, but sterile time and move us further toward meeting the person we are meant to be.

~ *Finding Meaning in the Second Half of Life*, p. 15

"Right relationship with the gods" as a psychological concept means that we harmonize our conscious life with the deepest powers that govern the cosmos and course through our own souls. Such moments of congruence will be felt as a sense of well-being, a reenergized relationship to self and world, and a feeling of "home" in the midst of the journey.

~ *Finding Meaning in the Second Half of Life*, p. 46

In examining that seeming oxymoron that a god, an eternal one, may die, he [Jung] explains that the name attached to a form may fade, but the energy behind it has only been transformed and reappears elsewhere.

~ *Finding Meaning in the Second Half of Life*, p. 161

The spiritual powers that the gods embodied, the invisible world made visible for a while, fall back into the human psyche and oblige humankind to suffer separation, alienation, and estrangement from them. Suffering this loss is then incarnated as personal or social pathology, because it is operating so unconsciously.

~ *Finding Meaning in the Second Half of Life*, pp. 161-162

Without a "vertical" sense of participation in divinity, humankind is condemned to a sterile, "horizontal" existence, circling its own absurdity and ending with its own annihilation.

~ *Finding Meaning in the Second Half of Life*, p. 164

The gods do not die, he [Jung] said, but the energy leaves their image; yet our clinging to the image, the old belief or dogma, causes the affect-laden experience to lose its power for us.

~ *Finding Meaning in the Second Half of Life*, p. 173

Our finite sensibility cannot ultimately know that infinite mystery that has been called *God*. We have, however, an experience of transcendence, and call it by the name *God*. But what we call God is not the name, not the image, but the profound energy behind the image, which gave rise to its numinous charge.

~ *Finding Meaning in the Second Half of Life*, p. 189

When the gods are not experienced as living, felt force fields of energy, then we will project outward and risk being owned by such numinous objects of our desire, or we will internalize them as somatic disorder or psychopathology.

~ *What Matters Most*, p. xiv-xv

. . . the metaphors of *the gods* are useful constructs, way of valuing, dramatic embodiments of the elemental energies of the universe, energies that have animated and driven life from the beginning and drive us all still today. They are the force fields that energize and move us toward their sundry ends beyond the powers of conscious comprehension, mythstreams in which we swim all the time. Why call them *gods*? Such a construct, such an expression, risks confusion with metaphysical reality, but herein the metaphor of *the gods* is simply meant to suggest immensity, endurance, significance, and our respectful acknowledgement of these large, transcendent energies that course through our histories.

~ *What Matters Most*, p. 45

Eros is the life force—*desire* that wishes most to connect, to build, to combine, to fuse, to generate with the other.

~ *What Matters Most*, p. 45

If the think of "the gods" as embodied energies, then we have not only a means of making such energies available to consciousness, but we offer our respect to the autonomy, transcendence, and omnipresence of those powers in our lives.

~ *What Matters Most*, p. 55

Let us remember that what the gods ask of us is that we remember them, respect them.

~ *What Matters Most*, p. 57

A god without mojo is dead, no matter how many priests, no matter how many parishioners, no matter how institutionally formidable.

~ *What Matters Most*, p. 105

Christ is not someone's name, not a noun, a fixed dogma or practice, but an energy, a current among many currents, which together and separately enact the mystery we call divine. The gods are not nouns, but verbs.

~ *What Matters Most*, p. 108

To be possessed by a complex is to have our ego consciousness owned by a split-off aspect of ourselves. To be possessed by a god, so to speak, is to be summoned to an obedience to something higher.

~ *What Matters Most*, pp. 115-116

When Nietzsche professed the death of God in the nineteenth century, he saw persons serving institutional forms, rote expressions, received confessions, ritualized behaviors, but no joy, no transformation, no mystery.

~ *What Matters Most*, p. 160

We can say that blessings may come to those who go through whatever miasmic swamplands the gods put in their way. They will have earned those blessings the hard way.

~ *Hauntings*, p. 132

So the gods have departed, left us to our own devices, and it's not going so well. We work assiduously at denial, convinced of our purblind assertions of certainty, partaking of a thousand distracting, numbing, addictive, seductive treatment plans that leave us so palpably alone, so lonely, and so terribly full of longing.

~ *Living Between Worlds*, p. 19

When one feels linked to the ancestors, or to the gods, or to the natural world, one feels at home, one's terror of extinction is subsumed in the great round of return to origins, but when one has suffered the erosion of those linkages, then one feels even more the cold breath of eternal night, and the urgency of those transient and momentary solaces of putative paraphilic connections—whatever form they take.

~ *Prisms*, p. 95-96

Chapter 10

Individuation

Individuation. The conscious realization of one's unique psychological reality, including both strengths and limitations. It leads to the experience of the Self as the regulating center of the psyche.

~ *The Eden Project*, p. 146

At no point do we live more honestly, or with more integrity, then when, surrounded by others yet knowing oneself to be alone, the journey of the soul beckons and we say "yes" to it all.

~ *The Middle Passage*, p. 94

To live a more abundant life we are obliged to understand the limits within which we were raised.

~ *The Middle Passage*, p. 94

The concept of individuation represents Jung's myth for our time . . . Individuation is the developmental imperative of each of us to become ourselves as fully as we are able, within the limits imposed on us by fate.

~ *The Middle Passage*, p. 97

... the individuation urge toward wholeness, obliges one to wait upon, and trust the guidance of, the soul's energies. The enemy of such trust is the anxiety occasioned by ambiguity. As one matures, a greater tolerance of ambiguity is essential both for growth and as a measure of respect for the autonomy of the mystery.

~ *Tracking the Gods*, p. 11

Surely the only measure by which we can judge ourselves in the end, or be judged by others, is the degree to which we have heard and responded to the imperative to become ourselves in the face of what would hold us back.

~ *Tracking the Gods*, p. 73

The meaning of our lives derives from the journey of individuation, which is intimately interwoven into the cosmic drama. . . By becoming oneself as fully as possible (which is what Jung means by individuation), one serves the larger purposes of history.

~ *Tracking the Gods*, p. 110

Setting out on the path of individuation, as easy and as obvious as it may seem, is an awesome task. It obliges leaving home psychologically, leaving behind the old comforts of place or person or ideology. It requires embarking on the journey toward the soul, a journey both joyous and intimidating. Often a cloud of undifferentiated angst seems to block the path.

~ *Tracking the Gods,* p. 137

As important as the task of individuating is in giving one a chance to operate more and more out of the natural self, and relieve in part the terrible feeling of inauthenticity, so individuation is equally critical to the quality of relationships with others.

~ *Tracking the Gods*, p. 138

[Four principles of relationships]
1. *One can achieve no higher level of relationship to another than one has achieved in relationship to oneself.*
2. *What we do not know or cannot face about ourselves, for example the mythologems (complexes) that drive and direct us, is projected onto others.*
3. *Power insinuates itself into all relationships.*
4. *Individuation is not self-indulgent but in fact enhances the quality of the self we bring to the other.* We love the other by lifting off him or her the burden of healing us and making our life meaningful. We free the other in proportion to the degree we have freed ourselves.

~ *Tracking the Gods*, pp. 138-139

The goal of individuation is not narcissistic self-absorption, as some might believe, but rather the manifestation of the larger purposes of nature through the incarnation of the individual.

~ *Swamplands of the Soul*, p. 14

The message of loss and grief and betrayal is that we cannot hold on to anything, cannot take anything or anyone for granted, cannot spare ourselves acute pain. But what abides is the invitation to consciousness. What is constant amid inconstancy is the summons to individuation.

~ *Swamplands of the Soul*, p. 51

Taking responsibility for one's journey is part and parcel of individuation. The individual's task is *to be* individual, to bring to fruition that experiment nature is making through us.

~ *The Eden Project*, p. 78

Relinquishing the expectation of rescue by the Other is one of the most difficult projects of our lives.

~ *The Eden Project*, p. 83

What courage it takes, then, just *to be*. Yet, it is in answering the summons to such a courage that we most help our partners. We relieve them of our impossible Eden project. We share with them the best person we can be—what a gift! And when we live our own journey, freeing our partners for the rigors of their task in life, then we most care for them, most honor them. This may properly be called love, though it is light years away from being "in love."

~ *The Eden Project*, p. 84

Implicit in the task of becoming conscious of wounded eros are certain questions which constitute an inventory of self and Other. If we do not ask them of ourselves, then our partners will, or we will hit some wall which obliges us to begin. Among them are:

1. Where do my dependencies show up in the relationship?
2. What am I asking my partner to do for me that I, as a mature adult, need to be doing for myself?
3. How do I repeatedly constrict myself through my historically conditioned attitudes and behavior patterns?
4. Am I taking too much responsibility for the emotional well-being of the Other? Am I taking on his or her journey at the expense of my own, and if so, why?
5. Am I living my life in such a fashion that I will be happy with the consequences of my choices? If not, when do I plan to start? What fears, lack of permission or old behaviors block me from living my life?
6. In what ways do I seek to avoid suffering?

~ *The Eden Project*, p. 99

The evidence is strong that there are no Magical Others, that we befoul our relationships with our own psychic debris, that the best relationship we can ever achieve with the intimate Other, and the Wholly Other, is a function of the relationship we achieve to ourselves.

~ *The Eden Project*, p. 138

Dialogue with the Other, however unpleasant or painful, is the catalyst for individuation.

~ *The Eden Project*, p. 140

It takes so damn much courage to be solely responsible for ourselves. And it is so often lonely.

~ *The Eden Project*, p. 144

The summons of the journey to embody one's story in the world requires a recovery of the largeness which our incarnation intends.

~ *Creating a Life*, p. 36

Unlike physical pain, which may be all too conscious, the pain of forced inauthenticity may remain unconscious, yet it engenders profound suffering which one may internalize as depression, externalize it as violence, anaesthetize with substances, or somaticize as illness.

~ *Creating a Life*, p. 45

The more one can align the world of conscious choice with the indications of the unconscious, the more one will feel a sense of personal harmony, whether or not one's choices are supported by the collective environment . . . in the end, such a choice comes down to whether one will give assent or not to what one is summoned to do by the Self. That summons is our vocation, the calling to become one-self, part and parcel of individuation.

~ *Creating a Life*, p. 46

If we are to assume that this is our life and not someone else's; if this is the only one we know we get; if choices are possible, and matter, then when do we plan to grow up, to take final responsibility for our lives? Who does not, in the end, want to believe that one *mattered*, that one's life counted for something?

~ *Creating a Life*, p. 48

Most often, the anxiety aroused by the summons to a larger life is more than we can bear.

~ *Creating a Life*, p. 49

To serve a construct which seems the product of one's life reflection, which finds feeling assent from within, which gives meaning and purpose to life, is to recover no small measure of personal freedom, dignity, and autonomy.

~ *Creating a Life*, p. 52

What kind of play has our life been, in service to what, or to whom? Do we like what we see, if we look honestly, and whose fault it is then? If we do not like what we see, then we are obliged to construct a fiction more worthy of service. If we are stuck, and know we are stuck, and we always do, then is there not some deep imperative to get unstuck? And is not the assumption of this responsibility for finding the right fiction to serve what we mean by "becoming something when we grow up"?

~ *Creating a Life*, p. 53

The resonance within us cannot be willed; it happens. No amount of willing will make it happen. But resonance is the surest guide to finding our own right path. It constitutes an inner guide amid imposing images of the outer world and the constant traffic of the intrapsychic world. Resonance is the deep resounding of our truth, when we find it, or it finds us.

~ *Creating a Life*, p. 61

Many of us have experienced our lives as guided somehow by some invisible agency.

~ Creating a Life, p. 68

Amor fati, the love of fate, is in the end a recognition that it is *here*, in *this place*, in *this time*, in *this arena* that we are called to live our lives. . . Loving one's fate, in the end, means living the life one is summoned to, not the life envisioned by the ego, by one's parents or by societal expectations. The love of one's fate is not fatalism, resignation, defeat or passivity. It is an heroic submission to the gods—not my will but Thine—which leads to the blessing of life lived as it was meant to be lived.

~ Creating a Life, p. 68

. . . individuation has to do with becoming, as nearly as one can manage, the being that was set in motion by the gods.

~ Creating a Life, p. 69

The love of one's fate is, finally, the affirmation that the gods are the gods, and that our task is to find their will, wheresoever that road will take us.

~ Creating a Life, p. 69

When Jung suggests that the greatest burden that child must bear is the unlived life of the parents, he is suggesting that wherever a parent was stuck in his or her individuation becomes an internalized paradigm for the child. That child *cum* as adult either replicates the pattern, overcompensates for it, or seeks to heal it in the outer life.

~ Creating a Life, p. 72

What is our duty to self and others? How are we to manage the competing claims of fidelity to relationship and summons to soul? These are the questions, part and parcel of individuation, that are to be lived, and continuously suffered, in the second half of life. The unconscious path of familiarity dooms one to living superficially. The conscious path of individuation means accepting the potentially creative tension of opposites, which inevitably involves a degree of crucifixion. To what do we owe our highest duty?

~ *Creating a Life*, p. 118

. . . we always know, somewhere inside, what is right for us. We may fear to know what we know, so its costliness persuades the ego to seek a thousand evasions; thus we dissemble, procrastinate, project unto others.

~ *Creating a Life*, p. 130

. . . individuation is a humbling task to serve what our deepest nature asks of us.

~ *Creating a Life*, p. 135

Just as vocation is found by serving one's *daimon*, so the meaning of our lives, our goal, is found in the movement of that energy. . . Naturally, each of us seeks the purpose of unique journey, and well we should. We betray the larger potential of our incarnation if we do not individuate.

~ *On This Journey We Call Our Life*, p. 114

. . . which hurt is greater—the angst-laden path of individuation in the face of the powerful environment, or the endless pain of the soul denied? What does matter, in the end?

~ *On This Journey We Call Our Life*, pp. 126-127

By whose authority do we live our lives, make our decisions, practice our professions, conduct our journeys? ...No child can ever wholly evolve into his or her own truth with finding an authentic inner authority. For this reason, the individuation process obliges some form of overthrow of the external authority, whether modeled by the personal parent, the broader culture, or the resident tribal deity. Much sentimentalization of the family and of tradition overlooks the fact that the individuation obliges some revolution, some transcendence of external authority to come to one's internal authority.

~ *Mythologems*, p. 47

Our duty is to risk living out our lives as fully as they [Jesus, Buddha] risked living their truths.

~ *Mythologems*, p. 61

It is part of our intuitive knowing as children that we were sent here with a story given by the gods. How we enact that story, suffering the various crucifixions of the ego's desire for comfort and security along the way, is what Jung means by the mythologem of *individuation*. Individuation, too often confused with individualism and with its attendant narcissism and self-infatuation, is rather more than an ordeal of summons, angst, false turns and humiliation before the gods.

~ *Mythologems*, p. 117

... individuation ... the lifelong project of becoming more nearly the whole person we were meant to be—what the gods intended, not the parents, or the tribe, or, especially, the easily intimidated or inflated ego.

~ *Finding Meaning in the Second Half of Life*, p. 10

While revering the mystery of others, our individuation summons each of us to stand in the presence of our own mystery, and become more fully responsible for who are in the journey we call our life. So often the idea of individuation has been confused with self-indulgence or mere individualism, but what individuation more often asks of us is the surrender of the ego's agenda of security and emotional reinforcement, in favor of humbling service to the soul's intent.

~ *Finding Meaning in the Second Half of Life*, p. 10

... all of us lack a deep sense of permission to lead our own lives. We learned very early that the world exacted conditions that, if not met, could result in punishment or abandonment. That message, overlearned and internalized, remains a formidable block to the ego's capacity to elect its own path. Only when the ego has reached a certain measure of strength, or perhaps more commonly, is driven by desperation to make a different choice, can we overthrow this tyranny of history.

~ *Finding Meaning in the Second Half of Life*, p. 13

In most lives, permission to live one's life is not something given; it is to be seized, if not in early ego election then later in desperation, for the alternative is so much worse.

~ *Finding Meaning in the Second Half of Life*, p. 13

The long-term neglect of the self will manifest somewhere, perhaps in physical illness, or depression, or more commonly in that crankiness that is the leakage of repressed anger. The difficult task is to balance one's own need for personal freedom and personal growth with the needs of others.

~ *Finding Meaning in the Second Half of Life*, p. 138

The task for each of us will be found in an increasing capacity to bear our lives without diversion and to suffer the soul's distress until we are led where it wishes to take us. Without more conscious suffering, we can never find depth or meaning, never really grow, and never really change our lives.

~ *Finding Meaning in the Second Half of Life*, p. 168

Personal authority. . . means . . . *to find what is true for oneself and to live it in the world.* . . . It is a humble acknowledgment of what wishes to come to being *through* us. . . . We all, privately, know this imperative summons every day, though we may flee from it: find what is true for you; find the courage to live it in the world; and the world will in time come to respect you (though at first you may confuse others and scare them).

~ *Finding Meaning in the Second Half of Life*, p. 184

We do not know who we are until we are obliged to reach deep within to draw upon the resources nature has given us.

~ *Why Good People Do Bad Things*, p. 198

Claiming our adult capacities, risking service to what wants to come into the world through us, is our individuation imperative. Setting forth upon the high seas of the unknown is where we are meant to be.

~ *Why Good People Do Bad Things*, p. 222

We are not here to fit in, be well balanced, or provide exempla for others. *We are here to be eccentric, different, perhaps strange, perhaps merely to add our small piece, our little clunky, chunky selves, to the great mosaic of being.* As the gods intended, we are here to become more and more ourselves.

~ *What Matters Most*, p. xiii

Living "large" is not narcissistic inflation, but rather encountered in the daily summons to risk being who we are.

~ *What Matters Most*, p. 63

Every one of us at some level knows what we want to do, need to do, have to do to live our lives.

~ *What Matters Most*, p. 119

Recovering our story, risking it, is what Jung meant by the *individuation* project. Because we get wrapped within our

99

provisional stories, the received scripts, we necessarily serve the compelling imagoes they embody. Archaic intrapsychic imagoes of self and other predispose us to repetitions in relationships. Or we bump up against the glass ceiling of familial limitation, the constricted imagination of complexes, or the constraints of tribal claim upon us.

~ *What Matters Most*, pp. 176-177

. . . most people, even those most accomplished outwardly, lack a core permission to live their lives; to feel what they feel, desire what they desire, and to pursue what their soul intends.

~ *Hauntings*, p. 111

Another far more subtle haunting is the refusal we all, in some form or fashion, have made of the gift of life, of the invitation to show up. When Jung formulated his concept of individuation he did not mean narcissistic self-indulgence—quite the contrary. Individuation is profoundly humbling. It obliges us to stand naked before the gift of life, the summons to personhood, and accede to the demand that we show up and contribute our small part to the big picture. From afar, that sounds reasonable, even doable, but in practice we all are intimidated by what it asks of us. Our well-being once depended on our fitting in, being adaptable, agreeable, accommodating. Individuation asks that we actually serve a separate summons to be different.

~ *Hauntings*, p. 138

Jung was right, it seems to me, when he claims that the individuation task is synonymous with, or analogous to, what our ancestors called a divine vocation: answering the summons of God. It obliges us to serve that which pulls us deeper than is comfortable, wider than is convenient.

~ *Hauntings*, p. 141

Of all these hauntings, the greatest is the one we alone produce: the unlived life. None of us will find the courage, or the will, or the capacity to completely fulfill the possibility invested in us by the gods. But we are also accountable for what we do not attempt.

~ *Hauntings*, p. 144

Finding personal authority requires two things: sorting through the traffic within and living what we find with courage and consistency.

~ *Living an Examined Life*, p. 21

For all the amends we owe this broken world, for all the recompense we owe others, we also owe ourselves permission to be who we really are, finally, before we are no longer here. We have to make amends to our soul for all the moments of complicity, cowardice, and co-optation that were once protective but now sour the soul and render it bitter.

~ *Living an Examined Life*, p. 27

What, then, is our task? Two things: individuation and overcoming the specific obstacles the fates have placed in our path.

~ Living an Examined Life, p. 40

. . . the meaning of our life will be a direct function of the degree to which we became more nearly ourselves, showed up as best we could in the face of the difficulties that life presented

~ Living an Examined Life, p. 42

The attainment of personhood is not self-aggrandizement; it is answering a summons to step into oneself, to honor one's interest, talents, and callings, whether recognized by others or not.

~ Living an Examined Life, p. 46

In all of these years, I have met only one person who had this sense of the large within her even as a child, and the courage to live it. She called this inner voice, this guiding genie, TWIHAT: an acronym for That Which I Have Always Thought. For reasons I do not know, this stalwart sojourner sustained a trust in that voice we all have within us. She trusted it, lived it, went through hard time with it, and came out the other side, as we all will if we risk trusting our own individuation process, our own guiding spirit, and our invitation to choose the large over the small. Then we serve not our egos, but our world, and bring a greater contribution to it.

~ Living an Examined Life, p. 49

Each of us has a gift, the essential gift of being who we are, with all the flaws, shortcomings, mistakes, and fears of which we are all so aware. . . In the end, we are not here to fit in, to be well adjusted, acceptable to all, or to make our parents proud of us. We are here to be ourselves.

~ *Living an Examined Life*, pp. 52-53

To be eccentric, not to fit in, to hear our own drummer, these are the signs of our bringing our gift, our personhood, to the table of life. It sounds so simple, but it is so difficult, not only because of all the disabling messages of the past but also because to be that gift asks us to let go and trust that something within us is good enough, wise enough, strong enough to belong to this world.

~ *Living an Examined Life*, p. 55

Individuation means submission, not ego triumph or transcendence of the ordinary. It means surrendering the life we wanted or expected, for that which the god or the soul (whatever metaphor you prefer) calls for.

~ *Living an Examined Life*, p. 67

. . . every day we are called to decide what kind of human being we will be. . . Individuation may be simply trying to show up as ourselves more days than not. All we are asked to do by history, the gods, nature, or by fate—whichever metaphor you prefer—is to show up as we really are. . . Individuation is the summons to grow up, to achieve personhood, to be a mensch.

~ *Living an Examined Life*, p. 101

It is not narcissistic to become—it is a duty.

~ *Living an Examined Life*, p. 110

So, what, then, was, is, *individuation?* Briefly put, it is incarnating the fullest possibility one can become, being less at odds with oneself, fulfilling the intent of nature, or the gods, a process far more likely achieved through natural unfolding than conscious intent or a conceptual grasp of Jungian principles.

~ *Prisms*, p. 153

The individuation process is an unfolding in service to a numinosity, a telos, an implicate destiny, a movement of the soul toward something indefinable yet compelling. When on track with this possibility, we are not spared suffering, nor do we win the plaudits of our tribe, but we may feel an inner confirmation, perhaps a sense of supportive energy.

~ *Prisms*, p. 154

Chapter 11

Initiation and Rituals

A *rite* is a movement in and toward depth. Rites are not invented; they are found, discovered, experienced, and they rise out of some archetypal encounter with depth.

~ *Under Saturn's Shadow*, p. 16

So, then, the double-edged sword of wounding. There are wounds that crush the soul, distort and misdirect the energy of life, and those that prompt us to grow up.

~ *Under Saturn's Shadow*, p. 64

Wounding has always been a crucial dimension of male initiation to adulthood, to sacred societies and even sometimes to profession.

~ *Under Saturn's Shadow*, p. 65

How difficult it is for men today who have no help across that great abyss. There are no rites, very few wise elders, and minimal modeling of mature male initiates. So most of us are left to our private dependencies, to swagger about in embarrassing macho compensation, or, most commonly, to suffering our shame and indecision in isolation.

~ *Under Saturn's Shadow*, p. 67

What the modern man most suffers from, then, is the wounding without transformation.

~ *Under Saturn's Shadow*, p. 75

The absence of meaningful rites of passage to manhood haunts their dreams. . . Again only by fidelity to the inner life, for instance by treating their dreams with respect, however unpleasant the message, will they be able to bring their secret fears to the light of consciousness.

~ *Under Saturn's Shadow*, p. 77

The uninitiated male hides his wound, his longing, his grief, a stranger to himself.

~ *Under Saturn's Shadow*, p. 91

The wounds men suffer today are not symbolic; that is, they do not transform. Because our culture lacks meaningful rites of passage, images that would activate and direct the energies of the soul, most modern men feel weighted, even crushed, by their roles and the expectations, outer and inner, upon them.

~ *Under Saturn's Shadow*, p. 106

. . . to define the hero as *one who expands our sense of the possible and yet reminds us of the necessary boundaries of the human condition.*

~ *Tracking the Gods*, p. 69

. . . the hero is always "called," although he or she may not initially understand this as a call or even wish to be called. . . Seldom is the way clear. . . Sometimes the hero will receive critical aid from another. . . If the hero survives the descent . . . and the battle with whatever monsters await in the depths, then he or she is able to undertake the ascent and be transformed. This transformation constitutes a death and rebirth experience. Who the person was, and what his or her conscious world was like, is no more. All is transformed. . . Wounds quicken consciousness and . . . are necessary quid pro quo for enlargement.

~ *Tracking the Gods*, pp. 71-72

While the journey of the hero may take the form of outer adventures, the goal is inner transformation. . . . the motifs of summons, descent, struggle, wounding, and return are part of the everyday life of the individual.

~ *Tracking the Gods*, p. 72

Adults too are missing initiated adults to whom they might turn. Most adult today are uninitiated, in that they have not experienced a death/rebirth, or found purchase in a larger vision vouchsafed by some wise elder who has been there and returned, compassionately, to share what is needed.

~ *Creating a Life*, p. 84

The absence of initiated mentors and wise elders is tragic, for it leaves subsequent generations bereft of that learning which is necessary to travel the world.

~ *Creating a Life*, p. 85

Just as we learn by going where we have to go, we learn most from those who teach us what we need, rather than want to know.

~ *Creating a Life*, p. 87

A sage is a person who has come to know what is true for him or her, one who has been refined by the fires of suffering and achieved a modicum of peace with what he or she knows, believes, lives. A sage is a person who has come to know one thing, and know it well, open still to growth, correction and change, and respectful of mystery, in whatever form it may appear.

~ *Creating a Life*, p. 88

The six stages of passage varied in form, intensity, duration, and cultural accoutrements, but essentially they were comparable around the world. They involved departure from home, not with an engraved invitation, not with a polite request, but suddenly and decisively. Second, there was a ceremony of death, ranging from being buried in the earth, to immersion, to an effacement of one's known referents. Third, there was a ceremony of rebirth because an emergent being, a differentiated psychology, was dawning. Fourth, they were given the teachings, in three categories: the archetypal stories of creation, of the gods, of the tribal history; the general roles and polity of adulthood in the culture; and the specific tools of hunting, fishing, child-bearing, and agriculture unique to that tribe. Fifth, there was an ordeal of some kind, often involving isolation in order that one learn to cope with fear and find internal resources. And sixth, after prolonged separation, there was a return to the community as a separated adult. Only in this way did young people transition from the naivete, dependency, and avoidance of childhood to the expectations of adulthood.

~ *Living an Examined Life*, p. 8

Chapter 12

The Journey through Life

. . . a need that typically arises in the second half of life: the need to redefine oneself, to relocate oneself in the context of a larger journey. If the purpose of the first half of life is to gather sufficient ego energy to leave home and set out into the world, the purpose of the second half is to align that ego with the grander energies of the cosmos.

~ *Tracking the Gods*, pp. 59-60

The archetype of the journey is the formalization of the life force.

~ *Tracking the Gods*, p. 75

For an age of wanderers, such relocation [in the divine drama] is the final homecoming. . . The memory of the Great Mother, her cycle of sacrifice, the great round, eternal return, serves both fate and the destiny of all humans. . . The other great idea, the hero's journey, reminds us of the counter truth that a person best serves the great mystery of nature by becoming an individual. The paradox is that a person must be subsumed into the great round and yet is incarnated here in order to differentiate and develop. In this

109

process the tribe is served, the individual is served, and, in ways we can only surmise, the divine is served.

~ *Tracking the Gods*, pp. 76-77

We are each obliged to suffer, to meditate upon, to incarnate, our unique experience of the cycle of sacrifice-death-rebirth, and, equally, to overthrow the gremlins of lethargy and fear to become that which nature so mysteriously offered. When we have taken on this unique yet absolute requirement that we become the protagonist in our own life drama, then we are living heroically.

~ *Tracking the Gods*, p. 77

Obliged as we are to live without absolute knowledge, to live with a burdening past that invades and disrupts our intentions in the present, and unsupported by the great mythic institutions of the past, we are called to relinquish the ego's need for certainty, and to experience, even enjoy, the ambiguity of our condition. At least, it is interesting. Accordingly, rather than say, "I am this construct, this ideology, this ego-identification," one may say, "I am my journey," or "I am my dialogue with the angels, the messengers of mystery." The widest opening to this mystery occurs at the point of greatest peril and pain. Where we most want knowledge is where we are most vulnerable. To risk that vulnerability, to embrace the ambiguity, is to be free and radically open to the mystery that animated the myths of our ancestors.

~ *Tracking the Gods*, p. 145

It is my belief that we would need to feel two things: that we had lived our own life as well and as fully as possible, and that we had some linkage with a larger order of meaning, some connection with the mystery that courses through history and animates the individual soul. These twin tasks—to live one's own life and to serve the mystery—are, paradoxically, aspects of the same thing, for the former obliges not only a willingness to accept responsibility for the course of one's life and for the meaning it embodies, but also the right to experience the absolutely different path it may take from those who have gone before.

~ *Tracking the Gods*, p. 149

To reach the end of one's life and to know that one has not truly taken the journey is more terrible than any terrors one would have had to face on the way.

~ *Tracking the Gods*, p. 149

. . . the goal of life is not happiness but meaning.
~ *Swamplands of the Soul*, p. 8

Indeed, next to the fantasy of immortality, the hardest fantasy to relinquish is the thought that there is someone out there who is going to fix us, take care of us—spare us the intimidating journey to which we have been summoned. No wonder we run from such a journey, project it onto gurus, never quite at home with ourselves.

~ *Swamplands of the Soul*, p. 11

What is not faced within is still carried as a deep personal pathology. To experience some healing within ourselves, and to contribute healing to the world, we are summoned to wade through the muck from time to time. Where we do not go willingly, sooner or later we will be dragged.

~ *Swamplands of the Soul,* p. 15

When I try to avoid my journey by transferring it to another, when I capitulate to the fear of loneliness, then I not only violate the unique meaning of my life which it is my summons to achieve, I also burden the one I profess to love.

~ *Swamplands of the Soul,* pp. 65-66

Jung noted, "Most of my patients knew the deeper truth, but did not live it." Which is to say, unless we live our deeper truths, we will spend many more seasons in Hell.

~ *Swamplands of the Soul,* p. 89

To go down into the anxiety state, to feel what we really feel, is to "go through" and break the tyranny of the timeless emotions that haunt us. We are Hell; unwittingly we have constructed it, and reflexively we serve it. The harrowing of Hell is the only way through to the aperture which Dante espied after his fearful journey. Only the descent into Hades can free us from Hades.

~ *Swamplands of the Soul,* p. 91

Who has not awakened at four a.m. to an encounter with the terrible truth that, history aside, we are to blame for what we have made of our life, for what we have become, for what we have done to others? We may experience these recognitions shamefully, with sadness or depression, but there is also a measure of self-directed anger there.

~ *Swamplands of the Soul*, p. 99

Many times the object of our fear is a symbolic representation for the anxiety that floats unnamed in the unconscious. . . the thing feared . . . symbolizes some deeper anxiety we have not made conscious, or perhaps some task we have not found the strength to take on.

~ *Swamplands of the Soul*, pp. 106-107

The more primal and reflexive such patterns are, the more we are their prisoners. Fears are normal and natural. Anxiety, which is a function of our personal history, is normal and natural. Angst, which is a consequent of the fragility of the human condition, is also normal and natural. What varies is the degree of affect and the nature and consequences of our responses. Since each of us has evolved reflexive responses to this anxiety, so we are in some profound and often unconscious ways prisoners of our own history. As our history and its responses remain powerfully programmed, whether we are conscious of this dynamic or not, so we collude in our repetitive wounding.

~ *Swamplands of the Soul*, pp. 114-115

Anxiety is the price of a ticket on the journey of life; no ticket—no journey; no journey—no ticket. We may run from anxiety as much as possible but we thereby run from our only life.

~ *Swamplands of the Soul*, p. 115

Again, no one is free who cannot say, with feeling, "I am not what happened to me; I am what I choose to become." "I am not my roles; I am my journey."

~ *Swamplands of the Soul*, p. 127

If we carry our Hell with us, and reconstitute it by our repetition compulsion, then we must also carry the Lord of the Underworld as well.

~ *Swamplands of the Soul*, p. 131

What happened to us, how we interpreted our experiences and internalized our understanding of it, is now rooted within us and causes us to reconstitute an ever-renewing Hell.

~ *Swamplands of the Soul*, p. 132

. . . three ideas of principles which . . . can lead us toward an enlarged psychic life. The first principle is that due to the natural ebb and flow of psychic energy we will inevitably and frequently be pulled down, against our will, into dark places. . . Thus it is essential for us to accept that *our psychic life will frequently act outside the control of the ego, that we will be pulled down into the swamplands, and that we will suffer there. . .* The second principle is that *in each of these swampland states there is an implicit challenge to discover its meaning and the change of behavior or attitude it may oblige.* Confronting each swampland as an implicit question—what is the meaning of my depression, to what is the anxiety linked in my history, what am I possessed by—allows us to be active instead of passive in our suffering. During this struggle we move from the fantasy of permanent happiness, or shame at not achieving it, to what is perhaps the greatest gift—the knowledge that we can live without happiness but not without meaning. . . The third principle animating this book is that *as our characteristic response pattern to swampland stress is reflexive in character, tied to past experience, we are obliged to re-imagine ourselves in order to live in the present.*

~ *Swamplands of the Soul,* pp. 141-142

Each of us has been offered a journey. Each of us is responsible for the fullest possible expression of this individuation imperative. While we need to do this work on a conscious, daily basis in any case, we may also choose to facilitate it with a therapist companion.

~ *Swamplands of the Soul,* p. 144

In the final analysis we do not solve our problems, for life is not a problem to be solved but an experiment to be lived.

~ *Swamplands of the Soul,* p. 146

The greatest gift to others is our own best selves. Thus, paradoxically, if we are to serve relationship well, we are obliged to affirm our individual journey.

~ *The Eden Project,* p 13

115

. . . all addictions are anxiety management techniques, seeking to lower the distress of disconnection through some actual or symbolic connection.

~ *The Eden Project*, p. 27

Projection, fusion, "going home," is easy; loving another's otherness is heroic. If we really love the Other as Other, we have heroically taken on the responsibility for our own individuation, our own journey.

~ *The Eden Project*, p. 57

To abandon the "going home" or Eden project is to open to the mystery of the encounter with the Other, to experience intimations of this great musician in whom and by whom we are held, and finally to free relationship for its highest service to us—the enlargement of our journey through the unfolding mystery of the otherness of the Other.

~ *The Eden Project*, p. 65

It is not whether or not one is wounded, but how deeply, and, more importantly, what adaptations we have made as a result. . . it is not life's inevitable wounding that damages relationships, but the precepts and stratagems we bring from our personal histories and impose upon the Other.

~ *The Eden Project*, pp. 76-77

The twin conditions for growth require first that we take responsibility for our journey. No matter what historic wounding, we must now and forever assume responsibility for our choices. Secondly, we must also be able to internalize, that is, be able to see that one's life is generated by choices whose dynamics derive from within.

~ *The Eden Project*, p. 78

We may offer each other encouragement, compassion, even great assistance, but we cannot take on another's journey any more than another can die our death for us. If they cannot die our death, why should they live our lives? Is not the meaning of being here tied to our becoming whatever the gods, or nature, intended?

~ *The Eden Project*, p. 83

The measure of our possible healing is the extent of our willingness and capacity to face such wounds, our unconscious patterns, our deepest desires.

~ *The Eden Project*, p. 89

But in the end, we, too, are required to pursue our own path toward wholeness. We carry forever the original woundings of eros, but as adults, we are responsible for those wounds, responsible for making them conscious, healing them, and thereby freeing ourselves and others from our pathology.

~ *The Eden Project*, p. 100

Surely the deepest wound of this world we inhabit is to feel uprooted from our divine beginning. It is one thing to wander as a hungry spirit, as we do; it is something worse to have forgotten that we carry the sacred energy within us, and are present to it, wheresoever we are. As transient beings we are nonetheless the carriers of the eternal.

~ *Archetypal Imagination*, p. 45

The ultimate end of depth psychology is to stand respectfully before inner truth and dare to live it in the world. What blocks each of us is fear—fear of loneliness, fear of rejection, and most of all, fear of largeness. We are all afraid to move from the confining powers of fate into the invitations of our destiny, afraid to step into largeness of our calling to be who we were meant to be.

~ *Archetypal Imagination*, pp. 103-104

What cannot be contained inwardly seemingly must be pursued outwardly.

~ *Archetypal Imagination*, p. 108

How hard it is to come to responsibility for our lives, to affirm that:

I am responsible for my history (at least after adolescence)

I am responsible for my personal well-being.

I am responsible for my individuation imperative, from which fear alone keeps me separated.

~ *Archetypal Imagination*, p. 117

Hubris is found in our capacity to convince ourselves that we really know what is going on. It is found in our capacity for self-deception, in the notion that we can choose with impunity, that we are in control, that we have covered all possible angles.

~ *Creating a Life*, p. 13

... *hamartia*, which has been translated as "the tragic flaw," but which I prefer to define as "wounded vision." Each protagonist believed that he or she understood enough to make proper choices, yet their vision was distorted by personal, familial and cultural history, dynamically at work in what we later called the unconscious.

~ Creating a Life, p. 14

We make our choices through *hamartia*, a wounded vision. The internalized phenomenology of childhood constitutes the lens through which one wanders the labyrinth of choice. Hence the paradox of the tragic vision is our common condition; namely, we have made choices for which we are responsible, choices which have hurt ourselves and others, and yet we did not know we were making flawed choices at the time we made them. Who rises in the morning, looks in the mirror and says, "I think I will do something stupid today"?

~ Creating a Life, p. 17

How humbled are we to find, in a thousand variations, that we have repeated our family's template, our old patterns in serial relationships, that we have embedded our unconscious tendencies in scene after scene. What the classical imagination expressed as the tragic vision remains profoundly true for us all, and helps explain why we suffer, and so often make a mess of our lives.

~ Creating a Life, p. 17

Paradoxically, where we may feel most frightened, or lacking permission, the ground for the greatest movement into meaning will often be found.

~ *Creating a Life*, p. 52

The test of a psychologically mature person, and therefore spiritually mature, will be found in his or her capacity to handle what one might call the Triple A's: anxiety, ambiguity, and ambivalence. . . The more mature psyche is able to sustain the tension of opposites and contain conflict longer, thereby allowing the developmental and revelatory potential of the issue to emerge. Anxiety arises in the face of uncertainty, open-endedness. Ambiguity confounds the ego's lust for security, to fix the world in a permanently knowable place. Ambivalence, the fact that the opposites are always present, visible or not, obliges one to deal with the capacity for dialogue with that other. This experience often obliges a confrontation with the shadow, where values rejected by the ego are not unlike exiles plotting to return home surreptitiously.

~ *Creating a Life*, pp 57–58

Fate is simply the word we have historically ascribed to whatever is given, unavoidably given.

~ *Creating a Life*, p. 65

The word character derives from the Greek *kharakter* which means a marking instrument; thus it denotes something engraved into the substructure of personality.

~ *Creating a Life*, p. 65

While we do not change past events, we do change their role, the effects of their programs in our lives, and how history plays out ever anew.

~ *Creating a Life*, p. 75

... the invitation of a crisis then is to sift through, to discern what is important, to find what developmental task may be required. . . Jung has observed that crises come at critical points in our life. Usually they make it painfully evident that the previous world-view or attitude of consciousness are inadequate to encompass the new situation.

~ *Creating a Life*, p. 76

Any crisis brings the limitations of conscious life to the surface and reveals the need for enlargement. . . we may well come to look upon it as a turning point, where our understanding grew, our psychology became enriched and differentiated, and our encounter with the unpredictable universe exploded into theretofore unimaginable new vision.

~ *Creating a Life*, p. 77

Anyone with a modicum of consciousness and a mild dollop of integrity will be able to enumerate a very long list of screw-ups, short-comings, betrayals, moments of cowardice and generalized incompetence. . . So accepting one's failings and limitations seems to constitute the most modest level of conscious endeavor.

~ *Creating a Life*, p. 89

It is easier to have poor self-esteem than it is to accept that our life is to be lived anyhow, in spite of, with all that risk, ambiguity, and then death at the end.

~ Creating a Life, p. 90

All of us have to learn to live with a sense of failure, the discrepancy between our aspirations and our accomplishments, between our hopes and our capacities.

~ Creating a Life, p. 91

Our journey through the dreck and dross of our messes is an invitation to an enlargement of soul. . . it is in the realm of mud and blood, defeat and despair, that the soul's fiber is fashioned. The mess of life is our mess. . . There is more mess of things to make ahead; some of them will be our great teachers, some will cause us to grow, and some will bring the fullness of failure to bear on the encounter with the mystery. Great meaning will often come from such dismal moments; they are our moments, our meaning, and we will be entitled to them because we will have paid dearly for them.

~ Creating a Life, p. 91

The old French maxim . . . (to understand all is to forgive all) suggests that if we truly knew the roots of each person's experience, and if all behaviors flow "logically" from their springs, we would be able to forgive them.

~ Creating a Life, p. 98

. . . living with mystery, with ambiguity, anxiety and ambivalence, is to my mind still a better living.

~ *Creating a Life*, p. 99

Find the secret sources of our distress, and being enlarged by the suffering of this conflict, is how we grow and mature. As Jung notes, "Suffering is not an illness; it is the normal counterpole to happiness." Our goal is not happiness, which is evanescent and impossible to sustain; it is *meaning* which broadens us and carries us toward our destiny.

~ *Creating a Life*, pp. 101-102

. . . symptoms are the critical road signs of our journey. . . All healing invokes Hermes, the god of crossings, for he bridges the known and the unknown and makes possible their reconciliation.

~ *Creating a Life*, p. 109

The capacity to love, in the face of the absurdities of our ends, permits us to live an enlarged life. Such a life will not be measured by its successes, but by the quality of its yearnings.

~ *Creating a Life*, p. 126

Living the symbolic life means that one has a sense of participation in a divine drama, an intuited connection to the forces which move nature and stir the blood.

~ *Creating a Life*, p. 129

Maturity, however, requires that we accept the largeness of our journey, and understand that we journey alone.

~ *Creating a Life*, p. 135

So, where are we then? On which road, the one that forever circles back to Thebes, or the one which leads to an unknown place, the place where we may meet the meaning of our journey?

~ *Creating a Life*, p. 151

The more we address the questions of our lives, the more we will experience our lives as meaningful.

~ *On This Journey We Call Our Life*, p. 16

The implicit question our family of origin lived became ours by internalization and assimilation, and, next to our genetics—also received from parents, of course—is the single most formative influence on our personal psychology.

~ *On This Journey We Call Our Life*, p. 17

We are all more than the sum of what has happened to us.

~ *On This Journey We Call Our Life*, p. 19

. . . we do not make our story; our story makes us.

~ *On This Journey We Call Our Life*, p. 22

Whatsoever we fear becomes the agenda for growth.

~ *On This Journey We Call Our Life*, p. 29

. . . what are the questions that might help us unravel this larger question: "By what truths am I living my life, or which are living me?. . .

- Where are your patterns?
- Where do you feel stuck?
- What anxiety is aroused when you contemplate alternatives?
- What specific fears can be unpacked from the much vaguer but paralyzing angst?
- Which of those fears is based on childhood experience, with its limited powers and its limited awareness of a larger world?
- Which of those fears are indeed likely to happen?
- Can you bear them happening?
- What will happen to you if you do not bear them, and you stay stuck?
- Can you risk being a larger person?
- Can you bear the pain of growth over the pain of remaining afraid, small, and lost?
- Can you accept that, at the end of your life, you were not really here?
- Can you bear to have been only a hungry ghost, a victim of fate, a refugee from destiny?
- Can you bear having been only a troubled guest on this earth without making some part of it yours?
- Can you face these questions?
- Can you live with yourself not facing these questions, now that you know they exist?
- Can these questions recover your journey for you?
- Can they, can you?

~ *On This Journey We Call Our Life*, pp. 33-34

A worthy fiction leads one to a worthy life. What fiction, then, is your truth right now, your guiding image? Is it worthy of the high summons of a life's journey?

~ *On This Journey We Call Our Life*, p. 85

So, what does one owe to the world? My own answer is: respect, ethical behavior and the gift of one's own best self. We serve others by becoming ourselves, what the gods intended.

~ *On This Journey We Call Our Life*, p. 91

If our personal psychology is fear based, as it often is, and denies our ultimate reality, how healthy can that be? What fine fruit falls from a poisoned tree? The building of empire, the expectations placed on partners and children for gratification, the flights into fantasy of immortality—all take us further from ourselves and whatever meaning we may chance to find in the fulfillment of our journeys.

~ *On This Journey We Call Our Life*, p. 101

Wherever we are stuck in our journey we bring hurt not only to ourselves, but to others as well. Doing our work thus becomes an ethical imperative, for it constitutes the chief good we can bring to those close to us. Doing our work requires accepting responsibility, finding the strength to pull our projections back from others, and engaging in a dialogue with the inner world whence our life choices come. That of which I am ignorant owns me, brings repetition and misery to my life and to that of others.

~ *On This Journey We Call Our Life*, p. 122

Asking the meaning of our suffering tends to relocate our sense of selfhood beyond the narrow purview of ego alone. Yes, it is a necessary tool of consciousness, but ego alone is insufficient. By submitting to something than itself, ego reframes experience to include far more than it can ever achieve on its own. That is why we pay attention to dreams. When psyche speaks it asks for enlargement, no matter how ambivalent we may be about that requirement. Wrestling with the angels of our darkness is what brings blessing in the end. We are meant to wrestle, not understand, not manage.

~ *On This Journey We Call Our Life*, p. 125

To ask, every day, "What matters, in the end?" is to create the possibility of differentiated choice, the potential to overthrow the tyranny of our history, so as to honor something in us that has always been there, waiting for our courage. If we limit our aspirations to good health and making money, then we might as well, in Jung's words, "quietly shut up shop." We may feel betrayed in doing so, but we will know who the betrayer is.

~ *On This Journey We Call Our Life*, pp. 128-129

. . . the purpose of therapy was rather to introduce one to a deeper suffering.

~ *On This Journey We Call Our Life*, p. 129

Suffering the tension between conflicting desires or needs or duties can lead to an awareness of what is really at stake in the context of one's larger journey.

~ *On This Journey We Call Our Life*, p. 130

What is alternative to banality, hysteria and consumerism? Is it not the honest, private suffering of the questions presented here? Who suffers his or her own personal journey will more honestly serve the world than do those who hew to a mass ideology, be it materialism, fundamentalism or nihilism. Any ideology denies the validity of the individual soul's journey.

~ *On This Journey We Call Our Life*, p. 131

So that is our life, with all its contradictions and conflicts, we somehow manage to endure. Suffering consciously is the only alternative to suffering unconsciously. It is a gift to oneself and, by lifting the burden off others, a gift to them as well. What we avoid in ourselves we load onto our neighbor. What we carry consciously ourselves, frees the other. No greater love, then, than sparing our neighbor, partner, child, by consciously accepting our own suffering.

~ *On This Journey We Call Our Life*, p. 132

No matter where I live, my journey is my home.

~ *On This Journey We Call Our Life*, p. 137

Risking compassion and imaging alternatives enlarges and deepens; it heals, always.

~ *On This Journey We Call Our Life*, p. 141

. . . compassion binds us with eros to this world, which is our home, and imagination creates a larger world, which is our destiny.

~ *On This Journey We Call Our Life*, p. 142

In the end we realize that our journey is our home, and the quality of that home is a function of the questions we ask. If our prevailing question is how to find security or acceptance, or how to avoid this journey, we will remain forever the lost children of our lost, frightened parents, drifting through our inner deserts. If our questions lead us to other more complex questions, we will find a deeper life, richer, more rewarding, more interesting and, most astonishingly, our own intended life, not someone else's.

~ *On This Journey We Call Our Life*, p. 143

In the end it is never about answers, which are always provisional and transitory. Rather it is about facing the challenge of the questions themselves.

~ *On This Journey We Call Our Life*, pp. 143-144

Living the questions, perhaps even learning to love them, keeps our life open-ended and therefore developing: they channel debilitating fear and vagrant desire into the progressive differentiated distribution of energy; and most of all, they make our life more interesting to ourselves and others. If we embrace what our Ithacas mean, then we are living in a respectful relationship with the great mystery that courses through us, rather than seeking reify and limit its potential.

~ *On This Journey We Call Our Life*, pp. 145-146

Our spiritual/psychological condition will never be cured, but it may be healed. Just as pain is physical, suffering is spiritual. Accordingly, we all experience the limits of our condition as a source of pain, but nonetheless must still wrestle with the Angel of Suffering to receive its blessing.

~ *On This Journey We Call Our Life*, p. 146

Troubling questions summon us to a larger life. In the meantime we walk, we all walk, in shoes too small. On the journey we call our life, we are best served not by answers which are but a seductive interregnum at best, but by questions which trouble us into growth. With conscientious struggle we may attain a larger life out of that trouble, and a death worthy of that life. . . Something wants to live through us, and we need to allow it. Whence and whither, this journey, is the question of questions.

~ *On This Journey We Call Our Life*, p. 147-148

Depth psychology supports a person's engagement with the mystery of his or her journey, seeks to support that person in an encounter with the invisible world which does manifest in the course of a process undertaken with courage, integrity and consistency.

~ *Mythologems*, p. 19

To not undertake our personal mission, then, is not only a failure of our own journey, but a failure for our culture. We live so much of our lives backwards, not only dominated by history, but through our backing our way nervously into the future. Little do we know that the future is waiting expectantly for us to become what we are destined to become when we have the courage to align our conscious choices with our individuation agenda. What blocks us is fear.

~ *Mythologems*, p. 68

To have gone to the mountain top, to have completed the ascent, one must finally discern whether one climbed the right mountain. The testimony of observers does not count. Only the confirmation of our quite separate psyches will suffice. When one reaches such a pinnacle of clarity, one may then be able to look upon the world with the keen eye, and perhaps even the detachment, of the ancients.

~ *Mythologems*, pp. 79-80

Our common condition is one of separation, the Fall, the loss, the expulsion from the womb, and the subsequent experience of a lonely, perilous wandering through an often hostile world, delaying only awhile the inevitable conclusion: annihilation. The desire for connection is symbolically transferred to food (matter/Mater), acquisitions, alcohol (the *aqua vitae* or *spiritus*), work, a warm body.

~ *Mythologems*, p. 107

The gods are present whenever we ask the right questions about our journeys. Knowing what questions matter is the first and nearly most difficult task. Living the questions the gods bring to us, in lieu of those we would prefer, is the greater challenge.

~ *Mythologems*, p. 148

The poet Dante began his famous, fabulous descent into the underworld with the recognition that midway in life he found himself in a dark wood, having lost his way. Despite our best intentions, we, too, frequently find ourselves in a dark wood. No amount of good intentions, conscientious intelligence, forethought, planning, prayer, or guidance from others can spare us these periodic encounters with confusion, disorientation, boredom, depression, disappointment in ourselves and others, and dissolution of the plans and stratagems that seemed to work before.

~ *Finding Meaning in the Second Half of Life*, p. 3

Most of us did not receive permission to take our journeys so seriously. Seldom if ever can we go back and obtain that permission. We have to seize it today from the depths of despair and doubt.

~ *Finding Meaning in the Second Half of Life*, pp. 73-74

What is not faced inwardly will play out in our external world; whatever burdens within will, sooner or later, burden without.

~ *Finding Meaning in the Second Half of Life*, p. 77

Growing up, leaving home, requires two practices. First, we must take responsibility for ourselves, and stop blaming others: the society, the parents, the partner, the malevolent gods. Secondly, we have to look within to see the repetitive core ideas, the complexes, and the historic influences where the true enemy lies.

~ *Finding Meaning in the Second Half of Life*, pp. 100-101

The chief disorders of our time are the fear of loneliness and the fear of growing up. The flight from loneliness drives people to mill amid malls, to stay in bad relationships, to abuse substances, and worst of all, to avoid a relationship with the self. How can we ever have a good relationship with another when we cannot have a good relationship with ourselves? The flight from ourselves will always mean that we will be uncomfortable with another. What we fear in ourselves we will fear in the other; what we avoid addressing in ourselves we will avoid in the other; where we are stuck with ourselves we will be stuck with the other.

~ *Finding Meaning in the Second Half of Life*, pp. 122-123

Growing up means takes psychological responsibility for ourselves, and not just economic and social responsibility—that is the easy part. Growing up means that we take spiritual responsibility for ourselves. No other can define our values, become our authority, or protect us from necessary choices. Until we accept this responsibility for ourselves, we are asking others to be a shelter for our homeless soul. As understandable, and universal, as that desire may be, remember that others will then be asking the same of us as well. How ingrown, and stagnant, such a relationship will prove to be. The immense soul that dwells within each of us will, in time. chafe and fret, and produce symptomatic messages of dismay. And in time, whether or not we stay outwardly bound together with a partner, we will psychologically leave the relationship by the diversion of Eros's energy to work, to another, to other projective possibilities, or invert it as depression or somatic illness.

~ *Finding Meaning in the Second Half of Life*, p. 123

Many of our lives are governed by guilt. If one can be conscious enough to recognize that attending to one's own needs is healthful and honest, and that drawing a boundary on someone else's demands is often necessary, then where is the offense? Guilt induction may be used by that dependent parent, even as they employed guilt earlier in life to control their offspring. If one is further conscious enough to recognize that guilt that compels compliant behaviors is really anxiety management, then perhaps one can stand up to the anxiety and be the only adult on the scene, the only one capable of knowing when enough is enough.

~ *Finding Meaning in the Second Half of Life*, p. 139

Meaning is found, over the long haul, through the feelings of rightness within. No one can give that to us, although we may allow others to take it away from us.

~ *Finding Meaning in the Second Half of Life*, p. 157

Where we relinquish hope for connection, for depth, for meaning, we find only sensation, and therefore we must do more of it, more often. We have a familiar, ugly name for this phenomenon and it is *addiction*. The culture of sensation can only produce addiction and broken hopes, just as fundamentalism can only produce rigidity and a very large shadow, as so many clergy scandals illustrate.

~ *Finding Meaning in the Second Half of Life*, p. 166

This task of becoming psychological in our outlook is very difficult, for it asks a leap of faith, an act of existential trust.

It asks nothing less than *to intuit and to value the invisible world that courses beneath the physical.*
~ *Finding Meaning in the Second Half of Life*, p. 177

If we are free from suffering, we are less likely to engage with those questions that ultimately define who we are. The rigor and depth of questions raised by suffering jar us out of complacency, out of casual reiterations of untroubled life, and bring us to the daily dilemma of enlargement or diminishment.
~ *Finding Meaning in the Second Half of Life*, p. 210

The failure to accept ourselves makes it very difficult, if not impossible, to accept others, despite our desire to do so.
~ *Finding Meaning in the Second Half of Life*, p. 221

No one is free of addictions, for addictions are anxiety-management techniques the purpose of which is to lower the level of psychic distress we feel at any given moment, whether we are conscious of the distress or not.
~ *Finding Meaning in the Second Half of Life*, p. 227

Anxiety is free-floating, unattached not unlike the fog that obscures the road we drive. Fear, however, is specific and if we can convert our anxiety into specific fears we will have taken a powerful step. . . To see in the cloud of anxiety the specificity of a fear, to confront the fear as an adult, is to break the tyranny of anxiety.
~ *Finding Meaning in the Second Half of Life*, pp. 230-231

If we look hard enough, we will find anxiety, or its management, at the root of so much we do. It is disconcerting to realize this fact, but in recognizing the ubiquity of anxiety in our lives and in those around us, we may feel greater compassion for ourselves and for each other. Philo of Alexandria is reported to have said, "Be kind. Everyone you meet is carrying a big problem." If we can accept that about ourselves and each other, accept the normality of anxiety, seek the roots of identifiable fears in the anxiety, then simply do the best we can and forgive the rest, we may at last become less anxious.

~ *Finding Meaning in the Second Half of Life*, p. 231

Life is not problem to be solved, finally, but a series of engagements with the cosmos in which we are asked to live as fully as we can manage.

~ *Finding Meaning in the Second Half of Life*, p. 232

The flight from the swamplands of the soul, however unpleasant they may be to consciousness, is the flight from the wholeness of life, a wholeness that may only be expressed in paradox, and any psychology or worldview that excludes paradox is excluding half of life itself.

~ *Finding Meaning in the Second Half of Life*, p. 233

When we recognize that we *are* a truth, a truth meant to be lived, a truth the denial of which harms not only ourselves, but others as well, then we are more inclined to speak directly and candidly.

~ *Finding Meaning in the Second Half of Life*, p. 248

It is rumored that the secret of the universe was once imparted by Hermes Trismegistus (Thrice-Greatest) in ancient Egypt. That secret . . . is that "things above are copies of things below, and things below are copies of things above" and "the way up and the way down are the same."

~ *Why Good People Do Bad Things*, p. xii

What I deny within will sooner or later arrive in my outer world. The more I am able to identify what works within, the less likely this material will need be played out in the outer world.

~ *Why Good People Do Bad Things*, p. 22

Both outer reality, neglected or devalued, and inner reality, neglected or devalued, will exact their due. Whether outer or inner, what we resist will persist and demand an accounting sooner or later.

~ *Why Good People Do Bad Things*, p. 56

The paradox that each of us must face is that to really grow up, to really leave home, one needs to separate from the parental imagoes and to begin to own some portions of one's own rich Shadow.

~ *Why Good People Do Bad Things*, p. 57

The only way to break the stranglehold of an addiction is to feel the pain that it is a defense against, a pain that we are *already* feeling.

~ *Why Good People Do Bad Things*, p. 68

Dependency is not love; it is dependency—it is an abrogation of the essential responsibility of each of us to grow up, to assume full responsibility for our lives. Not to take on this challenge is a flight from adulthood, no matter how mature a person may be in other areas of endeavors.

~ *Why Good People Do Bad Things*, pp. 95-96

Growing up means owning our vulnerability and learning to function in the face of it.

~ *Why Good People Do Bad Things*, p. 106

The examined life will oblige us to consider that all issues, *all* issues, have more than one facet to consider, that our capacity for self-delusion is very strong, that *we* are always at least part of the problem, and that we will ultimately walk right into what we have fled, sooner or later. What is wrong with saying, "I do not know; I do not possess certainty; I think this is a fascinating journey and I am open to discovery?" What should this simple confession require so much courage?

~ *Why Good People Do Bad Things*, p. 201

We are here to meet our summons, *our summons*, on this road of personal brokenness, doubt, despair, defeat, cowardice, and contradiction, with only scattered moments of luminosity.

~ *Why Good People Do Bad Things*, p. 234

. . . we all transfer the irruptions of the past into the conduct of daily life; we all suffer the fallacy of overgeneralization—

what was true then, or apparently true, is repeatedly ratified, reinforced by what is re-experienced—and unwittingly re-recreated in each new venue.

~ *What Matters Most*, p. 6

Learning that fear governs our lives, and the many coping strategies we have evolved to manage it, may be an unpleasant discovery, but it is the beginning of liberation. All it takes to recover the integrity of our journey is to recognize that fear is the enemy. . . As Jung observed, the spirit of evil is negation of the life force by fear. Only boldness can deliver us from fear, and if the risk is not taken, the meaning of life is violated.

~ *What Matters Most*, p. 11

In the end, we all fear two things, two categories of existential vulnerability: the fear of overwhelmment and the fear of abandonment.

~ *What Matters Most*, p. 12

Fear is the enemy. Life is not your enemy; the Other is not your enemy; fear is the enemy, and fear has crowded you into a diminished corridor of that vast mansion of possibility that the gods provide us. Ask yourself of every dilemma, every choice, every relationship, every commitment, or every failure, "Does this choice diminish me or enlarge me?"

~ *What Matters Most*, p. 13

... now you know your task: to become what the gods want, not what your parents want, not what your tribe wants, but what the gods want, and what your psyche will support if consciousness so directs... The meaning of our life will be found precisely *in our capacity to achieve as much of it as possible beyond those bounds fear would set for us.*

~ *What Matters Most*, pp. 14-15

As a species, we ill tolerate ambiguity, contradictions, or whatever proves uncomfortable, and that is what makes the anxiety-fueled "fundamentalist" in each of us take over from time to time. When that nervous part prevails, we violate the complexity of life, serve regressive strategies, narrow and diminish the journey life asks of us.

~ *What Matters Most*, p. 20

Our maturational process is directly linked to the capacity to progressively handle ambiguity, discomforting as it may prove.

~ *What Matters Most*, p. 26

An ability to tolerate the anxiety generated by ambiguity is what allows us to respect, engage, and grow from our repeated, daily encounters with the essentials mysteries of life... Certainty begets stagnation, but ambiguity pulls us deeper into life. Unchallenged conviction begets rigidity, which begets regression; but ambiguity opens us to discovery, complexity, and therefore growth. The health of our culture, and the magnitude of our personal journeys, require that we learn to tolerate ambiguity, in service to a larger life.

~ *What Matters Most*, p. 27

In the journey each of us lives, Eros is the guide of the quickened soul. Most of us learned early to distrust our desire, shy away from the large task that stands before us. Generally we seek comfort over enlargement, reassurance over risk, and seldom venture out beyond the predictable. Our dilemma is not that we are capable of both so much evil and so much self-denial, but that we are capable of so much spiritual pettiness. It may prove a "terrible" thing to be summoned before the large, before the call of the numinous, but it is in those moments that we express our journey most fully.

~ *What Matters Most*, p. 60

No matter how much we may have attained in the world, we are often stunned to realize that we may have lost contact totally with who we are, that is, whomever the gods intended.

~ *What Matters Most*, p. 65

Still another way in which we refuse to step into largeness is by holding on to the past, especially the limiting past. We hold on to grudges, slights, injuries, past wounding and allow them to dominate our present.

~ *What Matters Most*, p. 68

Until we grow up and step into the large challenge of living our journey as individuals and as a society, we will get the demagogic leaders and the infantilizing culture we deserve. These external artifacts reflect what we have not addressed within.

~ *What Matters Most*, p. 71

All of us have to ask this simple but piercing question of our relationships, our affiliations, our professions, our politics, and our theology: "Does this path, this choice, make me larger or smaller?"

~ *What Matters Most*, p. 71

As we get to this point in our life we see that stepping into a larger life is intimidating because it requires that we risk being who we really are, that is, what wants to come to the world through us, rather than serving our ego comforts or whatever instructions came our way. We cannot expect someone else to give us permission. The parent complexes, the culture complexes, are embedded in history, and never will stop saying what they always said. (They possess a stunted imagination.) So, it is up to us at this later point, when we have served those voices so long, to realize that our own psyches have a unique point of view, that each of us is different, and are bound for different destinies. Even siblings are bound for separate journeys, and all of us, at the end of our life, will have to answer as to what we did with our summons.

~ *What Matters Most*, p. 75-76

Choosing to risk one's own authority, to step into this fearful place, to realize through experience, that one will be supported by something deep within each of us, is what brings us home to ourselves.

~ *What Matters Most*, p. 78

. . . what we have become is frequently the chief obstacle to our journey. What we have become is typically as assemblage of defense mechanisms and anxiety-management systems generated by the adaptive needs that our fate-fueled biographies bring to us.

~ *What Matters Most*, p. 88

What we may also not have considered along the way is that every time we have shunned our summons to creativity, left undeveloped a talent or capacity, we have thereby removed that gift from the world. Our gift to the world is honored by bringing our best self to it; paradoxically, we do that by sacrificing ego comforts to our creative process, which, killing off the old, drives the project that we are forward.

~ *What Matters Most*, p. 125

By considering life absurd, we are obliged to make choices, real choices with real consequences, and thereby are the active agents in creating and affirming our value system. The more consonant these value elections are with our inner lives, our souls, the more meaningful we will experience these choices, and the more we will feel supported from within.

~ *What Matters Most*, p. 147

We all receive maps: this is what life is about—do this, do that, don't do this or that; value this, pursue that; count on this; avoid that, and so on. Received maps come from parents, religious and educational sources, popular culture, and from history. Sometimes these maps are helpful and rewarding, and sometimes they are not.

~ *What Matters Most*, p. 149

Every life is an enactment of stories, the sum of which is our biography, our resume, our epitaph. But the story we tell ourselves, or others, is only the story of which we are conscious. Our more enduring, more pervasive stories rise from deep, very deep archetypal matrices, genetic predispositions, cultural forms, intergenerational messages, sundry reflexive, reactive readings, and acquired defenses amid a world essentially unknowable, sometimes hostile, from which we do not escape alive. Nonetheless, we are called to achieve personhood—to contribute most to others by becoming who are, and standing for values that matter in this world, whatever obstacles history provides us.

~ *What Matters Most*, pp. 165-166

Thus the goal of an analytic therapy is not a "solution" to life's problems—were even a solution to exist—but to find one's story more interesting, to find that each of us is, after all, a character of great depth amid a deeply coursing drama, filled with life-defining choices presented on a daily basis.

~ *What Matters Most*, p. 167

The earlier the story, the more powerfully reinforced and the greater its staying power; the narrative wiring goes directly to our dank basement where catastrophic consequences retain their veto power.

~ *What Matters Most*, p. 178

Whatever our story may be, and that is for us to discover, it will require suffering, risk, anxiety, and often great loneliness.

~ *What Matters Most*, p. 180

"Going home" means paying attention to, respecting, the witness of these clues. It asks that we risk taking them seriously. It means tracking the clues to see where they wish to take us, which will not necessarily be where we wish to go. Going home means coming back to ourselves after so much estrangement.

~ *What Matters Most*, p. 182

Personhood is not a gift; it is a continuing struggle; the gift is attained later, and only from living a mindful journey where, prompted by an inner summons, we write our story at last.

~ *What Matters Most*, p. 185

Another way of looking at our life is to confess that we swim continuously in force fields of energy, our Greek ancestors called *Moira*, . . . or *Fate*. This is the energy of finite creation, with all its limits, boundaries, confines. You are born a certain person, with a genetic code, a set of parents, a cultural context, a zeitgeist, and in significant proportion are defined and delimited by these realities. At the same time, you swim in a force field they called *proorismos,* or *Destiny,* which is an expanding field of possible outcomes. Destiny encompasses whatever is capable of becoming.

~ *What Matters Most,* p. 190

Meaning is found both through the acceptance of fate *and* in the struggle to remain free, to make value choices amid a constricted range of possibilities. Whatever the gods do, we are still summoned to continue to be the guardians of our souls.

~ *What Matters Most,* p. 206

Loving one's Fate means that we live as fully as we can the life to which the gods have summoned us. We are not here to imitate those who have gone before, for that was *their* life, someone else's journey. We are here to figure out and serve what life asks of *us.*

~ *What Matters Most,* p. 209

. . . it is clear that those who fail to risk being who they are, who shun diving into the journey, are the most fear-ridden, regretful, and recriminating. With such a compromised purchase on their own history, they blame others, castigate themselves, or live with debilitating regrets. This is a bad way to go.

~ *What Matters Most,* p. 221

Our histories embody a paradox that humming beneath all our lives is a strange rhythm of *exile* and *homecoming*.
~ *What Matters Most*, p. 237

If we do not render our exile conscious, we burden our partners with inordinate expectations; we are prone to lives of distraction or superficiality; and we adopt beliefs that offend reason and daily experience in service to the comfort of facile promises—whether political, social, economic, or theological—that ultimately leave us dissatisfied and anxious.
~ *What Matters Most*, p. 238

. . . stages in our common developmental journey: call, exile, and homecoming.

1. *One is called to the next stage, to a task. . .* This "call" may not come as an angelic message in a dream, but can manifest as symptomology: boredom, panic, depression, or desuetude.
2. *The task that each of us is to address is different. . . individuation*, the summons to individual person-hood.
3. *Such tasks pull us out of our comfort zones.*
4. *We risk inflation in these moments.*
5. . . .the kingdom is ill because *some value has been lost, neglected, repressed, or forgotten.*
6. *Flight from this restorative task, as well as the honest experience of exile, will bring the retribution of "the*

gods." What is denied of the gods will always oblige them to reassert their imperative in forceful terms.

7. *The pathology that arises from any flight from the task is necessary to get our attention.* Pathology has to hurt enough to call us back to our task, to recognize the wrong turn, and to get on a different road.

8. *Suffering is the requisite for consciousness and recovery.* But suffering is always humbling. Humbling always brings us back to ourselves, for no one can live it for us or remove it from us.

9. *Homecoming is the goal, but our "home" is not "out there," a geographical place, the protective "other," or a comforting theology or psychology.* Homecoming means healing, means integration of the split-off parts of the soul, means redeeming the dignity and high purpose of our soul's journey.

~ *What Matters Most*, pp. 238-242

What gives us our journey also gives us our home, our richness, our meaning.

~ *What Matters Most*, p. 255

The challenge to each of us is to accept the danger of our personal journey and thereby accept the gift of our lives.

~ *What Matters Most*, p. 256

In the end, having a more interesting life, a life that disturbs complacency, a life that pulls us out of the comfortable and thereby demands a larger, spiritual engagement than we planned or that feels comfortable, is *what matters most*. To have been here, to have wrestles with such things, to have lived such questions, to have kept the mystery before us, to have joyfully accepted being "defeated by ever-larger things," to have kept one's appointment with destiny, to have taken one's journey through this dark, bitter, luminous, wondrous universe, to have risked being who we really are, is, finally, *what matter most.*

~ *What Matters Most*, p. 256

Synchronicity is a manifestation of energies moving through the invisible world and entering the visible world as seeming coincidence.

~ *Hauntings*, p. 20

How can one go wrong in humbly asking the questions, "Of what should I be mindful here. . .?" *Synchronicity* is merely a word that asks us to consider that there are . . . more things in heaven and earth than we had heretofore considered.

~ *Hauntings*, pp. 21-22

Life brings us two gifts: a moment in time and the consciousness of its brevity. We owe life two things in return: a life fully lived, and the gift surrendered at the end.

~ *Hauntings*, p. 28

Possibly the most subtle haunting of our lives is the unfinished business of the past.

~ *Hauntings*, p. 37

We have to learn to forgive ourselves for we have such ghostly hauntings because we have history, and history writes its message deeply into our neurology and our psychology. In workshops on various subjects I have often asked the question, "Where are you stuck in your life?" Nowhere . . . has anyone asked me "What do you mean *stuck?*"

~ Hauntings, p. 47

But *we are not our history;* ultimately, *we are what wishes to enter the world through us,* though to underestimate the power of that history as an invisible player in the choices of daily life is a grave error.

~ Hauntings, p. 53

How unpleasant to realize that finally we all have to face what we fear? All of us. How unpleasant to realize that until we do, the life we are living is at least partially in service to the dictates of the past, the persistent, interfering ubiquity of which cannot be exaggerated. Discerning these presences with their urgent, redundant messages is only the first step. But we will not even take that first step until we have to, until it costs too much not to.

~ Hauntings, p. 65

. . . the cost of a burdening past is guilt, and the cost of an uncertain future is anxiety. Each affective state, guilt or anxiety, has the capacity to erode our participation in the moment and remove us from the instinctual guidance in service to agendas of the past or anticipations of the future.

~ Hauntings, p. 67

Many of our behaviors, conscious or unconscious, are driven by guilt, shame, anxiety, and other dismal denizens of the soul. Typically, guilt shows up in our lives in one of three ways: patterns of avoidance, patterns of over-compensation, or patterns of self-sabotage. . . there are at least three modalities of guilt, all with very powerful claims upon our emotional lives. They are:

1. Legitimate guilt as a form of accountability for our choices
2. Contextual guilt
3. Illegitimate guilt as a form of anxiety management

~ Hauntings, p. 68

The ability to own our guilt, to acknowledge our shadowy capacity for wrong of all kinds, paradoxically allows us to move in new ways into the world. The trick is not to be defined by that guilt and its compensatory or evasive agendas, but to admit the wounds and flaws that characterize our species.

~ Hauntings, p. 70

Guilt as a defense against the archaic agendas of angst reflects the necessary conditionality every child faces, and it shows up later as a tacit lack of permission to be oneself. The only way one can recover traction on the present is to ask the question directly: "Of what (or of whom) am I afraid in this moment?"

~ Hauntings, p. 75

Guilt is . . . a confession of something one has done or failed to do. Shame is the belief that who one is is wrong, who one is is profoundly flawed. Shame comes from two major sources, the first being the belief that we have to meet some criteria, measure up, serve some demanding program, even be perfect. . . Other shame comes from the internalization of "assignments," both spoken and unspoken, from parents and others.

~ Hauntings, p. 78

So many adults, many of them highly accomplished in the outer world, suffer from a lack of permission to really be themselves, to feel what they really feel, desire what they really desire, and strive for the life that really wishes to be expressed through them.

~ Hauntings, p. 79

In the face of compelling guilt and belittling shame, what chance does a person have to breathe free and stretch wings of possibility? No chance, unless he or she suffers through to knowledge, to understanding, and outgrows these constrictive templates. It is easy for anyone outside these individual frames of experience to see what another must do and how easily it seems done. But then, reader, ask yourself where you are blocked, stuck in your development, confounded by your desires and bound by your restrictions, You may be certain that the binding agent for you, as for all of us, will be anxiety. While the specific components of the anxiety will vary for each of us, you may also be certain wherever guilt or shame are present, and they most always are, the strength to take on what needs to be done is sapped by these pernicious presences. Anxiety binds us to a possible future, and guilt and shame bind us to a constrictive past.

~ Hauntings, p. 80

How often do we allow the wounds and disappointments of history to define us and enable that diminution to persist in its wounding ways?

~ Hauntings, p. 91

If we are not willing to risk all, again, then we are precluded from intimacy. . . The paradox of the betrayal/trust dyad is that each is presupposed by the other, each needs the other to be real. Without trust, no depth; without depth, no true betrayal. . . To forgive is to recognize not only the flawed humanity of the other but our own as well, and in the end it is the only way to free the shackles of the past which binds us.

~ Hauntings, p. 95

But it is always easier to blame the other than recognize at how many stages of the process we betrayed ourselves, sustained denial, and perpetuated what was already outlived.

~ Hauntings, p. 101

We have all forgotten what our presumptive saints, mystics, and prophetic voices earnestly proclaimed: if we wait upon the dark, it grows luminous; if we abide the silence, it speaks. We look to others to fix it all for us, and they fail us, because we have asked too much of them, because they are broken themselves, and because we have ignored, even fled, our own resources. No wonder we find it so difficult to love others when we have seldom learned to love ourselves in a form which serves neither narcissism nor self-denigration.

~ *Hauntings*, p. 108

How scary it might prove to conclude that I am essentially alone in this summons to personal consciousness, that I cannot continue to blame others for what has happened to me, that I am really out there on that tightrope over the abyss, making choices every day, and that I am truly, irrevocably responsible for my life. Then I would have to grow up, stand naked before this immense brutal universe, and step into the largeness of this journey, my journey.

~ *Hauntings*, p. 109

. . . each of us, then, is left to answer these really important, and very personal questions:

1. How do you find true north in the conduct of our journey?
2. Do you know that you have an inner compass and how to access it?
3. Have you learned to trust it and to converse with it?
4. Do you know that your compass goes with you wherever you travel?
5. How do you plan to consult it more often in the conduct of your life?

~ *Hauntings,* p. 114

The old French proverb that to know all is to forgive all would challenge us to hear the story of the other in his or her faltering journey or, failing that, to at least understand that the other has a such a story which would, upon our hearing, melt our icy hearts and fear-driven defenses.

~ *Hauntings*, p. 117

How do we accept, finally, that we are not our history but our unfolding journey?

~ *Hauntings*, p. 119

Surely we have all tried, and continue trying, to fine tune the operations of our lives, but suffering awaits no matter what choices we make. The suffering of authentic choices, however, at least gives a person a meaning, which the various flights from suffering we undertake deny. One form of suffering enlarges, one diminishes; one reveres the life which wishes to be expressed through us, and one colludes in its sabotage.

~ *Hauntings*. p. 129

. . . we know we are stuck, and in every case we are stuck not because we lack knowledge, but because getting unstuck stirs the archaic fears within each of us and shuts the necessary change down.

~ *Hauntings*, p. 131

. . . the message that we are here to be *here,* to go through it all, and retain our dignity, purpose, and values as best we can. That is all we can do, and all that life can ever ask of us.

~ *Hauntings*, p. 133

Nietzsche's odd paradox has it right. We have to walk out into that abyss of the unknown and find that something supports us even when nothing supports us. In continuing to undertake that risk there is more spiritual freedom, more amplitude of soul, than we could have ever imagined. But that is where we are meant to be, living not as fugitives, but as mariners on a tenebrous sea, going through to a richer place.

~ *Hauntings*, p. 133

Who will ever tell the mystery of it all or name the ghosts which haunt us, drive us, impel us forward? Is not this life a series of repetitions, a set of variations, a series of investigations, experiments, and pummeling by the past? Bent forward, creatures of desire, driven by teleological urgencies, we seek our story amid the many stories that drive, surround, and overwhelm us. Much good work awaits us. It is our work, our lives, and we are responsible for it.

~ *Hauntings*, pp. 147-148

The moment we say, "I am responsible, I am accountable, I have to deal with this," is the day we grow up, at least until the next time, the next regression, the next evasion.

~ *Living an Examined Life*, p. 10

Sooner or later, we are each called to face what we fear, respond to our summons to show up, and overcome the vast lethargic powers within us. This is what is asked of us, to show up as the person we really are, as best we can manage under circumstances over which we may have no control. This showing up as best we can is growing up. That is all that life really asks of us: to show up as best we can.

~ Living an Examined Life, p. 11

Ask yourself these simple questions: Where do I need to grow up, step into my life? What fear will I need to confront in doing so? Is that fear realistic or from an earlier time in my development? And, given that heavy feeling I have carried for so long already, what is the price I have to pay for not growing up?

~ Living an Examined Life, p. 12

Where we find patterns, we also will likely find core, emotion-laden ideas within us, ideas that may or may not be conscious, may or may not be accurate, may not even be ours but have been part of our formative experience and the primal atmosphere we inhabited.

~ Living an Examined Life, p. 14

. . . letting go of the old is not easy. It requires being able to tolerate the aroused level of anxiety that besets any of us when ego consciousness is not in control. It requires that we let go of what we thought certain and cast our lifeboats upon a tenebrous sea. The more we resist change, the more we are allied against the nature of nature and the developmental agenda of our own psyches. Being aligned against our own nature is the very definition of neurosis.

~ *Living an Examined Life*, p. 16

Whatever health and wholeness is, it surely involved aligning our outer choices with our inner reality. When the path we are on is right for our souls, the energy is there.

~ *Living an Examined Life*, p. 23

Only in those moments when we take life on, when we move through the archaic field of anxiety, when we drive through the blockage, do we get a larger life and get unstuck. Ironically, we will then have to face a new anxiety, the anxiety of stepping into a life larger than has been comfortable for us in the past. This growth itself can be so intimidating that we often choose to stay with the old stuckness. We have to want something, really want it. We have to risk feeling worse before feeling better, and we have to risk the loss of the oh-so-comforting misery of stuckness.

~ *Living an Examined Life*, p. 38

Jung observed that usually behind the wounds lies the genius of the person. That is to say, where we are hurt often quickens consciousness and resolve and abundant energy to persist, even prevail. The key is not what happens to us but how it is internalized and whether those messages expand or diminish our resilience.

~ *Living an Examined Life*, p. 51

Recognizing the patterns, especially the self-destructive patterns, is the first step. Then comes taking them on, for the rest of one's life. Taking them on requires risk, courage, perseverance, and showing up more days than not. Some days the possibility of a larger life wins; other days the ghosts win. One has to know that every day is a war between the constrictive colloquies of history and the invitation to the high seas of the soul. But such a venture is what our life is about, what real adulthood is about, and what the journey of the soul demands.

~ *Living an Examined Life*, p. 62

So, what did we leave behind? For most of us, we left natural talents and enthusiasms behind for all sorts of reason, including social conditions such as poverty, lack of education, and constricted opportunities. Many of us left behind joy, spontaneity, creativity, and enthusiasm, given the battering that so many acquire along this journey we call our life. For some, they are very specific talents, callings, curiosities, but the "permission" to pursue them seems abridged at best and missing at worst.

~ *Living an Examined Life*, p. 76

In the end, we are haunted by the examples of the past, the denied permission to live a free journey. We are haunted by the partial examples of those in our purview, taking their pusillanimity or oppression as predictive of our own. We are haunted by social constructs that tell us what a woman is and what she can or cannot do, and what a man is and how he will be shamed by living beyond these calculated constrictions. We are haunted by bad theology, bad psychology, and bad social models into thinking we are defined by our history, by our race, or by cultural heritage. We are haunted by the unexamined lives of our ancestors and caregivers. We are haunted by the widespread impression that history is the future, And even more, we are haunted by the small lives we live in the face of our immense possibilities. Haunting is individual, generic, cultural, and extremely hard to challenge because it so often seems bound by generations of practice, ancestral fears, and archaic defenses of privilege.

~ *Living an Examined Life*, p. 85

The biggest haunting of all . . . is the specter of our unlived life.

~ *Living an Examined Life*, p. 86

If we live in haunted houses, we are called to turn the lights on and clean house.

~ *Living an Examined Life*, p. 86

If we are to grow up, we have to take on the invitation to self-determination, dialogue with the inner voice, answer the summons to an authentic journey—all quite contrary to the instruction to fit in. Growing up means, among other things, that I am accountable for my life, my choices, my consequences.

~ *Living an Examined Life*, p. 112

What we need to know is already known within. . . While we have hitherto noted that much comes between us and what we know, still our bones know, our blood knows, our dreams know, and sometimes we have to reach a point where we can no longer not know what we already know. And then it is possible life opens us before us, waiting only for our courage and resolution, waiting only for us to suit up and show up at last.

~ Living an Examined Life, p. 113

In childhood, simple questions led to simple answers. Because the large questions led to ever-larger uncertainty, many of us shut down, stopped asking, and thereby stopped growing. But the same questions are still being asked in the unconscious: *Who am I? Who are you? What is this all about? Whither are we bound, and how am I to live my life?* When they percolate to the surface, they bring each of us a summons. The only question is: Will we keep the appointment? Many, perhaps the great majority, never keep the appointment, never show up, and they lead lives of quiet desperation, suffer anesthetized souls, and have to continuously palliate distracted consciousness, Other show up because they have to. Keeping the appointment is where our lives find their purpose—not in the answers but in the living large questions that are worthy of the soul's magnitude.

~ Living an Examined Life, p. 118

Undertaking a dialogue with our own depths brings greater purpose, dignity, gravitas, and meaning in this journey we call our life.

~ *Living Between Worlds*, p. 27

We often stay stuck because ego consciousness is so easily distracted or lulled by the shabbiest of excuses or seduced by the flimsiest of strategies. And the stuckness persists. Accordingly, the only way through these dilemmas is "through" them, which is precisely what our protective mechanisms are trying to protect us from experiencing.

~ *Living Between Worlds*, p. 39

All of our anxieties, the existential threats to our well-being, can be catalogued under the twin categories of over-whelment and abandonment.

~ *Living Between Worlds*, p. 41

. . . in our forensic investigations of the "stuck places," we have to ask ourselves: *What anxiety will be generated here if I stop being stuck? Will I have to face something that feels overwhelming to me and step out into the world to take it on?*

~ *Living Between Worlds*, p. 42

When we are doing what is right for us, something inside us supports and carries us through even the most grueling, difficult times of our life. We all have had that experience of getting through a difficult place and being rewarded by the sense of rightness, the sense of purpose, the experience of meaning that rose from that place.

~ *Living Between Worlds*, p. 56

Even when the decision has been made in the deepest realms of our soul, the executive function of the ego is often intimidated, and we collude with our stuckness. As miserable as we may feel in the hole we have dug for ourselves, we choose to stay there for a very long time. At first, our plight arises out of our unconsciousness, and then out of our flight from knowing what we already know, and then from our failure of nerve to move into the unknown future. To reach the future, which is just as real as our past, we have to consent, or be driven, to be out of contact with the old for a very long time. No ocean is ever crossed without the willingness to risk, to leave behind the known shoreline long before the new land is found.

~ *Living Between Worlds*, p. 65

So too, we must also remain stuck unless and until we find the secret logic of our stuckness and face the anxiety that getting unstuck will bring to us when the resistance is overcome.

~ *Living Between Worlds*, p. 73

As I reflect on the healing process, I think of the following seven general principles.

1. **We are equipped by nature to survive, live our journey, and become.**
2. **Because of our powerlessness, we must adapt, and so we create "stories" to help us understand.**
   Our "stories" arise from trying to make sense of our life, to make it predictable, perhaps more manageable.

3. **We become servants of and prisoners to our "stories."**

Given that our stories are efforts to interpret the world and make it more knowable and more manageable, we come to depend of them to carry us through ever-new situations. The good news rising from our stories is that often our "interpretative fiction" allows us to build on our knowledge, bind our days together, and have a reasonably coherent personality. The bad news is that those same stories also impose the paradigm, the limited and limiting lens of the former into the immediacy of the new.

4. **Without the gift of psychopathology, we would never be stunned into awareness of the need for reconsideration, and thereby perhaps transform to a larger "story."**

Psychopathology is a gift, then, because it gets our attention. It tells us that our soul is not pleased with where our energies are going.

5. **Psychopathology calls us to accountability to something larger than "palliative" care.**

6. **Our central tasks are recovery of permission, personal authority, and personal aspiration.**

7. **The project of growing up is to keep working to heal the splits within until we serve what I wishing to enter the world through us in the first place.**

If we are ever going to be true to our own voice, it has to be now, while there is still time.

~ *Living Between Worlds*, pp. 85-92

It is in those difficult times that the larger journey is forged in the alchemical smithy of the soul, a place where the heat grows until the lesser molecules transform and the larger emerge. From time to time, the will of the Self transcends the needs of the ego-world and often requires the sacrifice of our most cherished values. . . Those who have gone through that transformation have been to Hell and need not fear it anymore; they know that life will bring further tests but will not allow them to settle back into the old, familiar place. From that point onward, they live with a deeper integrity and are less and less defined by the old fears or the many hysterias found all around them. The price and the often grave consequences are compensated through a more profound experience of meaning, whether or not it is ratified by one's tribe. This is a step into our own journey that, sooner or later, we are all asked to take.

~ *Living Between Worlds*, p. 106

In the end, the challenge to any of us regarding this internal dialogue is whether we can learn to trust, over time, what comes from within; mobilize the courage to act on it; and stick it out until we come into some clearing in the woods and know, intuitively, that that is where we belong.

~ *Living Between Worlds*, p. 108

But, in time, as we have seen of life's other insoluble, we grow large enough to contain what threatened to destroy us. We are equipped for the journey. We possess the resilience of our ancestors who clung to this spinning orb, tumbling through measureless space, and we survive, rich for all that has accumulated on our journey. The hard times take their place alongside the good times. It is only when they are together that we experience the richness of this journey. Again, life is never about happiness; it is about meaning. And meaning is only found in the whole picture, not in the difficult portions edited out—as people often do in their online reports to the world.

~ *Living Between Worlds*, pp. 110-111

We get through hard times by going *through* them, as all those before us learned along the same road. Why should we think our path should be easier than what they walked?

~ *Living Between Worlds*, p. 111

While friends, partners, and associations with others can be supportive, challenging, and dialectically developmental, it is also true that we grow most when we are on our own, when we have to figure out our path, when we have to find the courage to live it. Staying plugged in, merging with others, surrounding ourselves with noise of all kinds—all are flights from being with ourselves.

~ *Living Between Worlds*, p. 123

. . . we need to find what supports us when nothing supports us—that is, when the experience of the loss of the other is upon us and we are flush with separation anxiety, rather than run to the nearest safe harbor, we sit with it and sit it out. During that time, we learn, often to our surprise, that something rises within us to support us. We will not perish, though we think we will. By bearing the unbearable, we go through the desert to arrive at a nurturing oasis we did not know was there.

~ *Living Between Worlds*, p. 124

But to take someone else's path, no matter how sincerely, is to be living someone else's journey, and not our own. We may think we have nothing to bring to the table, no chip to add to the great mosaic, but that is how we wind up undermining our summons to personhood.

~ *Living Between Worlds*, p. 134

In a world of unpredictable, uncontrollable change, only our relationship to our guiding instincts, only our internal compass, only our dialogue with our dreams and revelatory systems of response provide continuity. Any one of us who has a relationship to our inner life, our autonomous, supportive psyche, will ride the currents of social change, as well as of personal change, and emerge on the other side.

~ *Living Between Worlds*, p. 135

The experience of enduring meaning is not found in the precincts of pleasure, affluence, or achievement, as we once thought evident, but in surrendering to something developmental, redeeming, and enlarging, something coursing through us, something wishing embodiment *through* us.

~ *Prisms*, p. 4

Let us remember for a moment the difference between *fear* and *anxiety*. Fear is specific: the fear of fire, the fear of heights, and so on. Anxiety is amorphous, vague, abstract even.

~ *Prisms*, p. 33

Can you ask yourself:
- Am I *living* my life or not showing up at all?
- Is my journey diminished by fear and by my collusion with that fear?
- Is fear the *driver,* and do I learn from time to time to stand up and risk being who I am regardless of the cost, regardless of the voices calling me back to a fugitive life?
- Where do I need to stand up now? Show up now?
- Did I remember to love and serve those around me? (In Albert Comus' *The Plague*, the protagonist, Dr. Rieux says that sometimes the most decent thing to do is simply do your job, be counted on, show up where you are needed).
- Have I learned that I, too, am equipped for this journey, provided the same tools, same resilience, and same tenacity that pulled my ancestors through?

~ *Prisms*, p. 53

There is a wounded part in all of us, and there is a healing part in all of us. From those centers, whether we know it or not, choices rise, patterns begin, and the unconscious engines of choice create our histories.

~ *Prisms*, p. 55

Learning the terrible truth that every healer must learn to survive is critical and maddening: *We cannot fix anyone, except, perhaps, perhaps ourselves.*

~ *Prisms*, p. 62

As Jung put it once, behind the wound often lies the genius of the person.

~ *Prisms*, p. 67

. . . each of us has to learn *we are not what has happened to us,* attached as we are to our epiphenomenal stories. *We are what wants to enter the world through us.*

~ *Prisms*, p. 111

To the degree that any of us feels insecure, that insecurity will show up over and over and over in venue after venue.

~ *Prisms*, p. 114

Over eight centuries ago, the writer of the Grail legend noted that when each knight took off in search of the Grail, each one went to a place in the forest where there was no path, for it would be a shameful thing to take the path someone else had trod before. Before we can accompany people on their journey through their dark wood, we have to have undertaken our own.

~ *Prisms*, p. 151

Wherever our own courage and resolve to see it through flags and fails, we will fail our patient, for what we have most to share with them is not our learning or our techniques, but rather who we have become and what darkness we have faced in the world and in ourselves.

~ *Prisms*, p. 151

But encased in this rag/flesh and bone/cage the heart beats on. We are left with our humanity, our yearning for love, for divinity, for release, yet are returned finally to the heart that, thumping its disquietude still, opens to life, to death, and to the greatest mystery of it all.

~ *Prisms*, p. 166

The real question is: *What is worth your suffering?* If you run from that, you will experience a revolt from within, sooner or later. If you engage it, your life takes on richness. You are not flushed with happiness, which is transient in the best of times, but you are flooded with meaning. Meaning makes all things bearable.

~ *Prisms*, p. 180

But when it is our journey, not the one imposed upon us, something always rises to guide us through.

~ *Prisms*, p. 181

I think two things: first, that we had lived our lives, and not someone else's, which is more difficult that it seems, and second, that we stood in the presence of something larger than we, and in doing so lived a larger life than our intimidations, our fears, our examples from others, might have allowed. In that lifetime struggle, we will have found and served our personal myth, the one that brings us back to ourselves in a richer way, and one that brings us to our appointments with the soul. Paradoxically, keeping that very personal appointment is how we bring something valuable to others as well.

~ *Prisms*, p. 182

. . . the quality of our lives will be a direct function of the magnitude of questions we ask, questions we are summoned to pursue for ourselves. And we do have to ask them on our own because there is precious little in our culture that does not elevate and privilege the banal, the distracting, the trivial—all of which are affronts and diminishments to the soul.

~ *Prisms*, p. 188

Asking the Questions that Enlarge
1. *Where has fear blocked my development, kept me constricted, and still prevents me from risking who I am?*
2. *What unlived life of my parents am I still carrying and passing on to my descendants?*
3. *What, really, is my spirituality, and does it make me larger or smaller?*
4. *Where do you refuse to grown up, wait for clarity before risking, hope for external solutions, expect rescue from someone, or wait for someone to tell you what your life is about?*

~ *Prisms*, pp. 190-196

Chapter 13

Marriage and Relationships

The truth about intimate relationships is that they can never be any better than our relationship with ourselves . . . All relationships, therefore, are symptomatic of the state of our inner life, and no relationship can be any better than our relationship to our own unconscious.

~ *The Middle Passage*, p. 47

Each party is primarily in charge of his or her own individuation. Through their relationship they support and encourage each other, but they cannot perform tasks of development, or individuation, for each other.

~ *The Middle Passage*, p. 48

Radical conversation is what a long-term commitment is about . . . Only radical conversation, the full sharing of what it is like to be me while hearing what it is really like to be you, can fulfill the promise of an intimate relationship. One can only engage in radical conversation if one has taken responsibility for oneself, has some self-awareness, and has the tensile strength to withstand a genuine encounter with the truly Other.

~ *The Middle Passage*, p. 61

So we bring ourselves to relationship. With scant knowledge of ourselves, we seek our identity in the mirror of the Other, as we once did in Mom and Dad. With all the wounds of this perilous condition we seek a safe harbor in that Other who, alas, is seeking the same in us. With a thousand adaptive strategies derived from the fortuities of fated time, fated place, fated Others, we contaminate the frail present with the germs of the past.

~ *The Eden Project*, p. 32

If one has not in fact grown in the course of a marriage, it has been a dreadful disaster. Mere longevity in a marriage is not necessarily something to celebrate, for what happened to the souls of these individual along the way?

~ *The Eden Project*, p. 44

Nothing has greater power over our lives than the hint, the promise, the intimation, of the recovery of Eden through that Magical Other. . . The repeated loss of Eden is the human condition, even as the hope of its recovery is our chief fantasy. Yet, we all know that the Other, a simple, flawed human being just like ourselves, can never carry the full weight of our Eden project. Nor can we carry the Other's.

~ *The Eden Project*, p. 50

We live the symbolic life as a direct consequence of the quality of our dialogue with the world and with the cosmos. . . We are asked from birth to death to become as fully as possible that which we are capable of becoming. Living in a dialectic with you, I am then living the symbolic life, which is to say, a life in depth. . . The dialectic of relationship described here, this grand conversation, may indeed be the proper definition of "marriage." Many married souls do not have a grand conversation, and therefore have yet to experience the *hierosgamos*, the sacred marriage, which properly honors the other as Other and at the same time protects the absolute uniqueness of the individual partners.

~ *The Eden Project*, p. 59

We can bring no greater gift to any relationship than ourselves, as we are, singular in solitude.

~ *The Eden Project*, pp. 60-61

Thus, to open to the Other is also a willingness to open ourselves to the experience of suffering. . . To use relationship as an escape from one's personal journey is to pervert relationship and to sabotage one's own calling. To care for the other as Other is to open to pain as well as joy. Both emotions can be transformative.

~ *The Eden Project*, p. 64

When we let go of our projections, relinquish the "going home" project, we are free to love. When we are free to love, we are present to the mystery embodied by the Other.

~ *The Eden Project*, p. 64

The willingness to sacrifice ourselves for the well-being of another is transformative. . . The power of love is found most in its triumph over fear. Where fear prevails, love is not. Given the ubiquity of fear, the move to love is a considerable challenge. Only those who can face their fears, live with ambiguity and ambivalence, can find that personal empowerment which then makes possible love of the Other.

~ *The Eden Project*, p. 73

To allow the Other to be Other is not an easy task, but it is the only way to love them. This is true too of the gods, for we wish most from them.

~ *The Eden Project*, p. 133

Three major issues that a person seeking to be mature and responsible must address in the context of relationships:
1) *What am I asking of the other that I ought to ask of myself?*
2) *Where do I need to grow up in order to allow the one I love to be who he or she is?*
3) *Where do I need sustain, even suffer, ambiguity over the long haul, to allow the inherent truth of the relationship to emerge?*

~ *Creating a Life*, pp. 136-137

For any relationship to survive, one needs luck, grace, and patient devotion to dialogue. Luck because the world is replete with absurdities, variables, complexities, which have the power to destroy any of us anytime. . . Grace obliges the strength of character which enables us to forgive ourselves and others for stupidity, cruelty, ignorance, narcissism and inattentiveness. . . Patience is the necessary companion of grace. The work of relationship is never finished, vigilance never concluded, renewal never final. Patience means sticking something out because it is so important.

~ *Creating a Life*, p. 137

There is a paradox at the heart of all relationships. We cannot know ourselves without the dialectical encounter with others, an encounter which obliges us to define who we are, and then to grow by incorporating our experience of the other. Yet, we cannot find any relationship more evolved than the level of development we bring to it.

~ *On This Journey We Call Our Life*, p. 86

Finding the other in oneself involves a dialogue which may impede or improve the quality of relatedness to the outer other. . . Failing to find the other in ourselves, to experience our own unfolding mystery, our quirks, our shadow, our complexes, neuroses and asportations, is to fail to find the most interesting relationship of all. We always remain a mystery to ourselves, so we have a life-long agenda for growth and development. Whoever is bored has not yet awakened to the large drama that courses within.

~ *On This Journey We Call Our Life*, pp. 87-88

The mystery of relationship may be found, paradoxically, in the progressively deepening encounter with the unknown beloved we ourselves are, the stranger most difficult to love.

~ *On This Journey We Call Our Life*, p. 122

177

The quality of our relationships, the quality of our parenting, the quality of our citizenship, and the quality of our life's journey can never be higher than the level of personal development we have attained. What we bring to life's table will be a function of how much of our journey we have made conscious, and how much courage we were able to muster to live it in the real world that life has presented to us.

~ *Finding Meaning in the Second Half of Life*, p. 34

It is far easier to be disappointed in the other than to call ourselves to account... Married or not, in my view, the two chief causes of relational discord are imposing inordinate expectations on each other and transferring old baggage into the present, thereby burdening the fragile new relationship with too much history.

~ *Finding Meaning in the Second Half of Life*, pp. 105-106

When we look at this problematic question of falling in love, we see a number of implications emerge. First, what we do not know about ourselves, or do not wish to know, has a tendency to be projected onto our "beloved." Second, we have a predisposition to project our childhood agendas, our infantile longings, and the burden of our assignment for personal growth onto the other. Thirdly, since the other cannot in the end, and should not ever, carry the responsibility for the task of our life, the projections inevitably wear away and the relationship has a tendency to deteriorate into a power struggle... Fourthly, it only stands to reason, that the best thing we can do for ourselves and for the other is to assume more of the developmental agenda for ourselves.

~ *Finding Meaning in the Second Half of Life*, pp. 116-117

When we are able to sincerely ask the question "What am I asking of my beloved that I need to do myself?" we have not only begun growing up, but may then be expressing a loving attitude toward that other after all.

~ *Finding Meaning in the Second Half of Life*, p. 117

The inescapable truth of any relationship is that it can achieve no higher level of development than the level of maturity that both parties bring to it.

~ *Finding Meaning in the Second Half of Life*, p. 117

A more mature relationship is based on "otherness" itself, on the dialectical principle that demonstrates that my one and your one together create the third. The "third" is the developmental process that results as we influence each other in turn; we grow by incorporating that influence into our private sensibilities. We do not learn and grow by all subscribing to the same school of thought, copying the same values, or voting the same way. We grow from the experience of our differences, although in insecure moments we quickly forget this. The capacity to include those differences, even incorporate them into an ever broader more sophisticated range of choices, is the chief task, and gift, of an evolving relationship.

~ *Finding Meaning in the Second Half of Life*, p. 118

The more we wish another person to repair our wounds, meet our needs, and protect us from having to grow up, really grow up, the more dissatisfying the relationship will prove over the long haul. It will swamp in stagnation. If, however, we can see that the relationship is a summons to growth, in part by encountering the otherness of our partner, the relationship will support each person risking, stretching, and growing beyond the point where they entered.

~ *Finding Meaning in the Second Half of Life*, p. 120

Love asks that we confer on the other the freedom to be who they most profoundly are, even as we wish the same for ourselves.

~ *Finding Meaning in the Second Half of Life*, p. 121

Loving will ask that we assume the burden of our fearful agenda, replace our tentative, timorous tread with a bold step into life, and spare the other the task of taking care of us.

~ *Finding Meaning in the Second Half of Life*, p. 123

The more the family can tolerate divergence, and separate summonses to a larger destiny, the more each person will feel freed for his or her own growth. The more the family can affirm each member, child and parent alike, the greater the likelihood that love rather than perversions of power will prevail.

~ *Finding Meaning in the Second Half of Life*, p. 140

Most relationships, especially those most intimate, have an aura of disappointment about them, for we silently feel the other has betrayed us by not meeting our agenda for that relationship. . . such expectations are projections onto the other of our mislaid responsibilities for ourselves. We are always letting the other down, as they let us down, even when we both try not to. An awareness of this agenda, and its inevitable betrayal, can lighten relationships by bringing us to a more realistic appraisal of possibility, and a more responsible assumption of the task of our journey.

~ *Finding Meaning in the Second Half of Life*, p. 218

If we cannot bear being with ourselves, how is it that we ask another to do that for us? In fact, the capacity to be with ourselves, as we really are, finite, imperfect, and deeply flawed, will prove not only the "cure" for loneliness but our secret gift to others as well.

~ *Finding Meaning in the Second Half of Life*, p. 223

A relationship should serve the growth of each party toward becoming more nearly who he or he is capable of becoming.
~ *Why Good People Do Bad Things*, p. 95

. . . marriage is so typical because it carries, and suffers, the burden of our chief fantasy, namely, that the magical "other" will fix things for us, render life meaningful, heal our wounds, and help us avoid the task of growing up and facing the huge existential vacuum that all conscious souls must engage. Because life, with all its possibilities, all its decisions, is so huge, we cling to the small, and hope the

Other will spare us the task of growing up. But since they do not, cannot, and should not, we are angry with them. This is Shadow material, for it feeds on that which lies within us, that which makes us uncomfortable with ourselves, that which intimidates us.

~ *Why Good People Do Bad Things*, p. 97

A mature relationship is one in which each party assumes responsibility for her or his individuation, and supports the others in her of his as well.

~ *Why Good People Do Bad Things*, p. 99

In assessing the strength of the relationship, one is really asking the strength of the individual, whether they are mature enough to take on responsibility for their own lives.

~ *Why Good People Do Bad Things*, p. 100

Reluctantly, ineluctably, we are drawn to acknowledge three principles of relational dynamics, principles that are present in all relationships at all times:

I. We have a tendency to project onto the Other what we do not know about ourselves (the *unconscious*), or what we do not want to know about ourselves (the *Shadow*), or our reluctance to grow up and assume full responsibility for ourselves (our resistant *immaturity*).

II. Since the other will not, cannot, and should not take on the responsibility of what we have deferred—our unconsciousness, our Shadow, our immaturity—or our hidden agenda is frustrated, and the relationship tends to devolve into the problem of *power*, with its invitation to control or manipulate the other, or to *blame*, with its familiar dyad of victim and villain.

III. The relationship is thereby left with the choices of dissolution, blaming, sustained anger and depression, or growing up. The only way in which we can grow up, and the relationship evolve into a realistic experience worthy of our continuing investment is to withdraw the projections and transference over time, own them as our Shadow stuff, and take responsibility for our emotional well-being and spiritual growth, even as we choose to support our partner's efforts to do the same.

~ *Why Good People Do Bad Things*, pp. 104-105

Chapter 14

Men

The Eight Secrets Men Carry Within
1. Men's lives are as much governed by restrictive role expectations as are the lives of women.
2. Men's lives are essentially governed by fear.
3. The power of the feminine is immense in the psychic economy of men.
4. Men collude in a conspiracy of silence whose aim is to suppress their emotional truth.
5. Because men must leave Mother, and transcend the mother complex, wounding is necessary.
6. Men's lives are violent because their souls have been violated.
7. Every man carries a deep longing for his father and for his tribal fathers.
8. If men are to heal, they must activate within what they did not receive from without.

~ Under Saturn's Shadow, p. 11

The power complex is the central force in the lives of men. It drives them and wounds them. Out of their rage they wound others, and out of their sorrow and shame they grow more and more distant from each other. The cost of this mutual wounding is enormous, repetitive and cyclic. Whatever is unconscious is internalized in debilitating ways or projected onto others and acted out destructively.

~ *Under Saturn's Shadow*, p. 25

As Joseph Campbell expressed it, one can spend one's whole life climbing the ladder, only to realize that it had been placed against the wrong wall.

~ *Under Saturn's Shadow*, p. 101

Each father's son must ask himself, "What were my father's wounds? What were his sacrifices, if any, for me and others? What were his hopes, his dreams? Did he live out his dreams? Did he have emotional permission to live his life? Did he live his life or the Saturnian tapes? What did he receive from his father and culture that hindered his journey? What would I have liked to know from him about his life, his history? What would I like to know from him about being a man? Was he able to answer such questions, however tentatively, for himself? Did he ever ask them? What was my father's unlived life, and am I living it out, somehow, for him?

~ *Under Saturn's Shadow*, p. 119

A man must ask himself . . . What fear blocks me? What tasks do I, in my heart of hearts, know I must undertake? What is my life calling me to do? Can I bring my work and my soul closer together? How can I serve both relationship and individuation? What areas of father's unlived life must I occupy and plant my flag on?

~ *Under Saturn's Shadow*, p. 128

Being a man means knowing what you want and then mobilizing the inner resources to achieve it.

~ *Under Saturn's Shadow*, p. 128

No man may leave home or be in the world without suffering grievous wounds to body and soul. But he must learn to say, "I am not my wound or my defense against my wound. I am my journey."

~ *Under Saturn's Shadow*, p. 132

Chapter 15

Midlife

Midlife is an opportunity to reexamine our lives and to ask the sometimes frightening, always liberating question: "Who am I apart from my history and the roles I have played?"

~ *The Middle Passage*, p. 7

The Middle Passage is an occasion for redefining and reorienting the personality, a rite of passage between the extended adolescence of first adulthood and our inevitable appointment with old age and mortality.

~ *The Middle Passage*, p. 7

The invitation of the Middle Passage is to become conscious, accept responsibility for the rest of the pages and risk the largeness of life to which we are summoned.

~ *The Middle Passage*, p. 8

Most of the sense of crisis in midlife is occasioned by the pain of that split. The disparity between the inner sense of self and the acquired personality becomes so great that the suffering can no longer be suppressed or compensated. . .

The person continues to operate out of the old attitudes and strategies, but they are no longer effective.

~ *The Middle Passage*, p. 15

One is summoned, psychologically, to die unto the old self so that the new might be born. . . Thus, the Middle Passage represents a summons from within to move from the provisional life to true adulthood, from the false self to authenticity.

~ *The Middle Passage*, p. 15

Awakening to the Middle Passage occurs when one is radically stunned into consciousness.

~ *The Middle Passage*, p. 18

The Middle Passage begins when one is required to face issues which heretofore had been patched over.

~ *The Middle Passage*, p. 19

One of the most powerful shocks of the Middle Passage is the collapse of our tacit contract with the universe—the assumption that we act correctly, if we are of good heart and good intentions, things will work out. We assume a reciprocity with the universe. If we do our part, the universe will comply.

~ *The Middle Passage*, p. 41

Thus, apart from shock, confusion, even panic, the fundamental result of the Middle Passage is to be humbled.

~ *The Middle Passage*, p. 41

This is the one aspect of the appointment we have with ourselves during the Middle Passage: to reclaim those parts of ourselves left behind through specialization, ignorance or prohibition.

~ *The Middle Passage,* p. 77

Fear of our depth is the enemy. . . At midlife permission is to be seized, not requested.

~ *The Middle Passage,* p. 106

The experience of crisis at midlife is the collapse not of our essential selves, but of our expectations.

~ *The Middle Passage,* p. 115

After the Middle Passage, no one can say where the journey will take us. We only know that we must accept responsibility for ourselves, that the path taken by others is not necessarily for us, and that what we are ultimately seeking lies within, not out there.

~ *The Middle Passage,* p. 115

If our courage holds, the Middle Passage brings us back to life after we have been cut off from it. . . We may even come to realize that it does not matter what happens outside as long as we have a vital connection with ourselves.

~ *The Middle Passage,* p. 116

The crux of the middle passage is the requirement that a man, whatever his age or station, pull out of his reflexive

behaviors and attitudes, radically reexamine his life, and
risk living out the thunderous imperatives of his soul.

~ Under Saturn's Shadow, p 126

The two greatest fantasies we are obliged to relinquish in
the second half of life are that we are immortal exceptions
to the human condition, and that out there somewhere is
some "magical Other" who will rescue us from existential
isolation.

~ Swamplands of the Soul, p. 59

Depression at midlife is very common. It seems that there
is a necessary and inevitable collision between the false self,
reflexively cobbled together as a reaction to the vagaries of
childhood, and the natural self which wishes to express
itself.

~ Swamplands of the Soul, p. 71

Strange as it may seem, we have to invent a "second
adulthood" as a necessary fiction, even as the hackneyed
"inner child" was invented to acknowledge the power of
history. What was too large for that child is now the agenda
for the adult. The adult has greater ego strength, capacity
for reflection and objectivity, and alternative possibilities
unavailable to the child. What restrains is fear, for sure, and
the constraints of the imagination. None of us can escape
psycho-pathology, the ubiquitous wounds to the soul, and
the distortions of our natural paths which result. The
invitation is to summon courage to take on the world anew,
to relinquish outmoded identities and defenses, and risk a

radical imaging of the larger possibilities of the world and of self.

~ *Archetypal Imagination*, p. 118

...one of the chief signs of the shift into the second half of life is the move from the magical ideas of childhood through the heroic, necessary self-delusion of youth and early adulthood, to the sober experience of limitation and regret in later life. Few of us arrive at the second half of life with clarity, conviction, satisfaction, because life too often led one along a tortuous path, away from the road envisioned.

~ *Creating a Life*, p. 67

To have a hope of surviving the second half of life, one will have to find a measure of self-forgiveness. . . We are all worthy, as unworthy as we are, and are redeemed by our capacity to feel unredeemable.

~ *Creating a Life*, p. 79

This is the critical question of the second half of life. *What am I called to serve?* If the question is not asked consciously, we will be possessed by something, some unconscious value, some complex, some adolescent rebellion which continues unabated. If we ask the question consciously, we will have to ask it periodically, at different stages of life. An answer valid for one stage may be oppressive in another.

~ *Creating a Life*, p. 113

In time, we begin to recognize that the enemy, so to speak, and therefore the deliverer as well, is within. We recognize that the energies we have projected onto the world derive from inner scenarios, that we are makers of our world, and the whole second half of life stands as a summons to consciousness. This means that what is wrong in my life is in me; what is repetitively wounding is in me; what is healing in my life is in me. As obvious as this may sound, in daily life such a recognition is as profound as it is difficult to achieve.

~ *Creating a Life*, p. 132

... one ought to spend some part of every day of the second half of life in a profound gratitude.

~ *Creating a Life*, p. 147

The difficulties of creating a life are compounded by the power of the unconscious, early conditioning and the fragility of our consciousness and will. Yet, the whole purpose and dignity of our lives is directly proportionate to the degree that one takes on the great labyrinthine puzzle in the second half of life.

~ *Creating a Life*, p. 150

What are the questions we need to address? . . . psyche presents us with two large questions, one for the first half of life and one for the second. The question for the first half of life is essentially this: "What is the world asking of me?" . . . The question of the second half of life, however, is quite different: "What, now, does the soul ask of me?"

~ *On This Journey We Call Our Life*, p. 14

The second half of life may certainly still include goals, but hopefully more appropriate ones. They will prize depth over abundance; wisdom over knowledge; humility over arrogance; experimentation over security; growth over comfort; meaning over peace of mind.

~ *On This Journey We Call Our Life*, p. 100

Recall that the question of the first half of life is: "What does the world demand of me, and can I mobilize my resources in the face of fear and intimidation to meet those demands?" Just as surely the question of the second half is: "What does the psyche (soul) ask of me?" A full life requires that we suffer and struggle with both questions.

~ *On This Journey We Call Our Life*, p. 137

The second half of life presents a rich possibility for spiritual enlargement, for we are never going to have greater powers of choice, never have more lessons of history from which to learn, and never possess more emotional resilience, more insight into what works for us and what does not, or a deeper, sometimes more desperate conviction of the importance of getting our life back.

~ *Finding Meaning in the Second Half of Life*, pp. 9-10

The most common characteristic of this kind of passage [midlife], despite the different story we each embody, is the deconstruction of "the false self"—the values and strategies we have derived from internalizing the dynamics and messages of our family and our culture.

~ *Finding Meaning in the Second Half of Life*, p. 29

At this point in the journey, one is invited to experience deeper meaning in one's suffering, and to learn that something transcendent to the old way of being always comes when one has the courage to continue this journey through the dark wood.

~ *Finding Meaning in the Second Half of Life*, p. 29

Most of us live our lives backing into our future, making choices of each new moment from the data and agenda of the old—and then we wonder why repetitive patterns turn up in our lives.

~ *Finding Meaning in the Second Half of Life*, p. 31

But in the second half of life, the worm turns, the agenda shifts to reframing our personal experience in the larger order of things, and the questions change. "What does the soul ask of me?" What does it mean that I am here?" "Who am I apart from my roles, apart from my history?"

~ *Finding Meaning in the Second Half of Life*, p. 86

After midlife we are truly on our own, morally and psychologically responsible for the conduct of the journey, and not only the outer world but our psyche will hold us accountable. In the outer world we will have to deal with the consequences of our choices, clean up the mess perhaps, and in the inner world, we will suffer the dis-ease that arises from violating the agenda of the soul.

~ *Finding Meaning in the Second Half of Life*, p. 90

Only with insight can the second half of life have any real capacity for choice and for development beyond these recalcitrant powers of our history.

~ *Finding Meaning in the Second Half of Life*, p. 97

Standing up to our fear is perhaps the most critical decision necessary in the governance of life and the recovery of the soul's agenda in the second half of life.

~ *Finding Meaning in the Second Half of Life*, p. 98

Leaving family psychologically remains a separate, more critical, sometimes impossible task for the second half of life.

~ *Finding Meaning in the Second Half of Life*, p. 128

In the second half of life there are two major tasks: The first is *the recovery of personal authority. . .* The recovery of personal authority is a daily task imposed upon all of us by the soul. Closely allied with the task of gaining, or better recovering, personal authority is the task of *discovering a personal spirituality*.

~ *Finding Meaning in the Second Half of Life*, pp. 183-184

... the obligatory adaptations of the first half of life require a progressive diminishment of *personal authority* to the point that we cease to know who we are, apart from our roles and our history, lose contact with what we desire, and become strangers to ourselves. The critical summons of the second half of life is to recover a personal sense of authority, explore, thoughtfully express the personal Shadow, and risk living faithfully with the soul's agenda.

~ Why Good People Do Bad Things, p. 55

The second half of life is a summons to the life of the spirit, namely, to ask, and answer for ourselves, uniquely, separately, *what matters most*. When we resist the many deaths asked of us, we resist the summons into a larger life. When we resist engaging our fears in service to growth, we abrogate the will of the gods. The poet Rainer Maria Rilke said it best when he asserted *our task is to be defeated by ever-larger things.*

~ What Matters Most, p. 92

Finding what is true for oneself, and living it in the world, is surely the largest challenge of the second half of life. . .

~ What Matters Most, p. 155

Surely the supreme task of the second half of life requires taking on accountability for writing one's personal story and the acquisition of courage to live it in the world. . . the story the ego was living, the fiction it embraced, was not the true story, hence the deep sorrow, the nostalgia we all carry for a lost home. *That lost home is ourselves*. . . . we can only make it back home to ourselves by going forward into the unknown scary possibilities of a risky, more fully lived journey.

~ What Matters Most, p. 179

While the chief agenda of the first half of life is to develop an ego, a sense of self strong enough to leave parents, step out into the world, and create a provisional life, the agenda of the second half of life surely ask us to reconsider: Now, in service to what do I live my life?

~ *What Matters Most*, p. 207

As we have seen agenda of the first half of life is forged from suffering demands of all kinds and responding to the blows, challenges, and seductions of life, while the second half of life has more to do with the wrestling with the aftermath: guilt, anger, recrimination, regret, recovery, and the possibility of forgiveness of self and others. The former is one kind of struggle—mostly with the world—and the latter is mostly with ourselves and the questions of transcendent meaning that continue to perturb us.

~ *What Matters Most*, p. 251

The second half of life is not a chronological moment but a psychological moment that some people, however old, however accomplished, however self-satisfied in life, never reach. The second half of life occurs when people, for whatever reason—death of partner, end of marriage, illness, retirement, whatever—are obliged to radically consider who they are apart from their history, their roles, and their commitments.

~ *Living an Examined Life*, p. 20

Insight, courage, endurance—not a bad litany of which to be mindful every day. The days we remember and do our best—all that is ever asked of us—are days in which we reclaim personal authority from the vaults of history. Then we may know we have truly moved into the second half of life, the part where we get our life back.

~ Living an Examined Life, p. 24

In the first half of life, our summons is to build an ego strong enough to enter the world, deal with it, meet its demands, and create a living space for ourselves in it. This is seemingly what growing up requires and all life apparently expects.

~ Prisms, pp. 3-4

. . . I think the meaning of the entire second half of life, (second half used more metaphorically than chronologically) is about finding, or submitting to, something larger than our ego needs, something larger than our complexes with their insistent chatter. If the first half of life is about "*what does the world want from me, and how do I meet its demands*," the second "half" is about "*what wants to enter the world through me?*"

~ Prisms, p. 4

In book after book and therapeutic hour after hour, I have asserted that the primary task of the so-called "second half of life" is the recovery of "personal authority."

~ Prisms, p. 188

The agenda of the first half of life imposes adaptations of all kinds, and we all respond in our variegated ways to the demands, blows, challenges, and seductions of life, while the second half necessarily obliges sorting through the aftermath of choices and consequences: guilt, anger, recriminations, regret, recovery, and a summons to forgiveness of self and others. Thus, the second half of life is usually less a chronological event, a desperate resolve, than a persistently compelling subpoena to sort through that immense internal traffic we all carry and to discern what is true for us.

~ *Prisms*, p. 189

Chapter 16

Myth and Mythology

All mythology is a playing out of some variant of two great mythologems. The mythology of the Great Mother is the great circle, the death-rebirth motif, the Eternal Return. The mythology of the Sky Father is the quest, the journey from innocence to experience, from dark to light, from home to the horizon. Each mythic cycle must be served.

~ *Under Saturn's Shadow*, p. 84

Myth takes us deep into ourselves and into psychic reservoirs of humanity.

~ *Tracking the Gods*, p. 7

. . . the study of myth is the search for that which connects us most deeply with our own nature and our place in the cosmos.

~ *Tracking the Gods*, p. 8

The Greek word *mythos* means *word, story, speech*, related to the notion of expression. . . Myth, with its substance of symbol, rhythm and metaphor, bridges from the unknown to the Knower and helps the human stand in some sort of meaningful relationship to mystery.

~ *Tracking the Gods*, p. 8

To literalize a myth or a symbol and require its worship . . .
is the oldest of religious sins: idolatry.

~ *Tracking the Gods,* p. 9

*Myth is the dramatization of conscious or unconscious values
of a group or an individual . . .* anything that can carry the
imprint of divine energies can be a temporary vessel of the
mysteries, or the gods.

~ *Tracking the Gods,* p. 12

Joseph Campbell identified four ways in which myth serves
human need—to the cosmos, to nature, to each other and
to ourselves. *The cosmological question* . . . we ask, "How
did I get here? Who, or what, was here before, and will be
after? Why?" . . . The cosmological office of myth addresses
the questions of *ultimacy,* of genesis and eschatology, alpha
and omega. . . *The metaphysical question.* Metaphysics is
the effort to identify the nature of reality, especially the
nature of the world around us. . . *The sociological question* . . .
Who one is is in part defined by *whose* one is—to whom
or to what communal purpose one subscribes. . . Social
organization serves biological needs, for sure, but it also
serves the spirit. Meaning comes to the individual through
participation in the tribal experience. . . Three cultural
artifices are employed to seek reconnection with the primal
mysteries—dogma, rites, and cultic practices. *Dogma*
represents the afterthought of a people as they seek to
contain the mystery by the power of thought, by the
stratagems of scripture, theology and catechism. *Rites* are
symbolic reenactments of the primal experience. *Cultic*

practices help define the singularity of one group versus another by way they dress, interact, and incarnate their tribal response to the demands of everyday life. All of these are well-meaning attempts to sustain the primacy of original experience, but few survive the erosion of time. Thus dogma can evolve into assertions that neither touch nor speak to the subsequent generations. Rites can lose their exemplary power and luminosity. Cultic practices can deteriorate into habit, oppressive tradition, even a tyranny of expectations. *The psychological question* . . . How are we to understand ourselves as ourselves is the psychological task of myth. Literally, this means asking questions such as: "Who am I? How am I to conduct my life? What is my proper place in the world, my vocation? How am I to find a companion who is right for me?"

~ *Tracking the Gods*, pp. 13-17

The function of myth, therefore, is to initiate the individual and/or the culture into the mysteries of the gods, the world, society and oneself.

~ *Tracking the Gods*, p. 17

[Ten Different Approaches to Myth]
1. *Antiquarian.* This view of myth acknowledges our natural curiosity about other peoples, especially our ancestors.
2. *Sociological.* This reading of myth sees it as a carrier of the social values of a group.
3. *Historical.* The historical understanding of myth sees the narratives of gods and heroes as faded accounts of

real people and real events, however transformed through the alchemy of time, oral transmission, and imaginative embellishment.

4. *Proto-scientific.* Many understand myth as the inadequate reading of nature—what humans had before science.

5. *Anthropological.* The anthropologist is concerned with the origins and rise of human culture.

6. *Linguistic.* The etymological study of a word, concept or mythologem will often lend considerable insight into the root metaphor which arose to express the inexpressible primal experience.

7. *Psychological.* . . many students of myth have read them as a fascinating thesaurus of scenarios that dramatize the processes of psychological life. . . one may see the instinctual desires and value conflicts of the individual and often the tribe as well. This approach to myth understands it as a demonstration of the universality of psychological functioning.

8. *Archetypal.* . . certain motifs recurred throughout world culture and also in dreams and other psychic phenomena experienced by individuals.

9. *Phenomenological.* Myth is a form of radical apprehension. . . We experience phenomenologically, as felt movement of body and soul.

10. *Symbolic.* . . myth represents the crystallization of basic experiences of life construed through various forms of imagery. Such imagery lies beyond intellectual comprehension yet is experienced meaning. Mythic images help us approach the

mysteries. . . Reading myth, then, is a form of personal and cultural psychotherapy. . . The recurrent motifs of the myth constitute the movement of soul through the ages and through the life of the individual.

~ Tracking the Gods, pp. 18-23

If the purpose of myth is to connect us to the four orders of mystery, and if what we have available to our culture is simply one or another ideology—specifically materialism, hedonism, or narcissism—then the experience of modernism is the anguish of yearning from within our estrangement.

~ Tracking the Gods, p. 25

The questions, explanations and great rhythms that once guided the soul by way of living myth are still within us, still guiding our lives. And we are obliged to render this process more conscious lest we live blindly, false to ourselves and false to nature.

~ Tracking the Gods, p. 29

Historically myth springs autonomously from the deep unconscious, or out of a phenomenological encounter with transcendent personal or tribal experience.

~ Tracking the Gods, p. 29

Myth has always been the bearer of psychic values. With the decline of mythic sensibility, those values have withdrawn into the unconscious of individuals and the tribe, or it has been projected onto outer events and institutions.

~ *Tracking the Gods*, p. 51

The great paradigm shift that lies at the very core of modernism is the loss of mythic connection to the cosmos. The incarnation of meaning, once carried by myth and myth-sustaining institutions, has gone within, receded, as Jung said, from Olympus to the solar plexus, from worship to psychopathology.

~ *Tracking the Gods*, p. 53

. . . two important mythic patterns: the eternal return and the hero's journey. . . Historically, the myth of the eternal return was associated with Great Mother Goddess, and the quest was associated with the Sky Father, the solar hero.

~ *Tracking the Gods*, p. 53

To experience one's life in depth, as part of a larger context, is the central contribution of myth, which, as Jung points out, "explained to the bewildered human being what was going on in his unconscious." . . . Thus myth enables one to feel a sense of spiritual "locus," and presents images that support and direct transformative energies, lending coherence to the random chaos of life.

~ *Tracking the Gods*, p. 54

The eternal return is part of the cycle of sacrifice (*sacre + facere,* to make sacred), bringing new life through death, plowing under that life might burst forth anew.

~ *Tracking the Gods*, p. 55

The central mythologem of the goddess is the cyclic nature of nature—the seasons, the tides, the systole and diastole of the blood stream.

~ *Tracking the Gods*, p. 55

The experience of the goddess is threefold—maiden, mother, and crone, each representing a stage of consciousness and each a stage of natural development.

~ *Tracking the Gods*, p. 56

The central meaning of the experience of the Great Mother is the cycle of sacrifice. The truth the goddess embodies is that the life-death cycle is fed by sacrifice, that all life feeds on other life, and then serves to feed another. . . As goddess embodies all life, she must sacrifice all her children that life might grow. The sacrifice of the divine child is a recurrent motif in Western myth.

~ *Tracking the Gods*, p. 57

Myths tell us what is really going on both within ourselves and within the cosmos. As a seventeenth-century alchemical manuscript expressed it, "All that is above also is below."

~ *Tracking the Gods*, p. 61

Simply put, the purpose of the cycle of blood and sacrifice, death and rebirth, is to enable us to participate in the suffering of the elected one, and through that suffering to be lifted out of the random horrors of life into a mythologically appropriated plane of mystery and meaning.

~ Tracking the Gods, p. 63

If we live within a too narrow a myth, that is, a set of images provided by our culture or family of origin which constricts the health of the soul, we suffer that self-alienation we call neurosis.

~ Tracking the Gods, p. 64

The awareness that there is a depth dimension to all that we experience enlarges our vision, relocates us in a timeless zone. Participation in the great round retains both the mystery it represents and the dignity of those who die.

~ Tracking the Gods, p. 64

The cycle of sacrifice, which terrifies the ego, supports and heals the soul.

~ Tracking the Gods, p. 65

Psychodynamic therapies arose because of the erosion of the great myths and myth-sustaining institutions. . . the primary wound of modern individuals is often the wound to the soul.

~ Tracking the Gods, p. 79

Caring for the soul, attending to the deep wound to one's meaning, is what depth psychology is about. . . myth delineates the movement of soul.

~ Tracking the Gods, p. 126

Myth is not created. It is experienced as an energy of the cosmos, shaped and incarnated by the unconscious, received or ignored by consciousness.

~ *Tracking the Gods*, p. 148

The steady erosion of stabilizing mythologies has dimmed the inner longitudes and latitudes from which humans have drawn their bearings for centuries.

~ *Swamplands of the Soul*, p. 102

Myth is the invisible plane which supports visible conscious life. When we experience its presence, we feel grounded, connected.

~ *The Eden Project*, p. 135

. . . we read myth to learn what is in the human soul; we read the human soul to learn the dynamic laws and principles of the mythic cosmos.

~ *Archetypal Imagination*, p. 24

But healing requires that we become psychological, against our will in most cases. Our complexes, our neuroses, our personality disorders all derive from early or especially powerful experiences internalized as mythological systems. It is not that we live in a mythless age. We are all in service to those mythological imagoes, those charged value systems, those repetitive world views, which own us and drive us to serve history.

~ *Archetypal Imagination*, p. 116

"Myth," as it is used here, refers to those affectively charged images (imagos) which serve to activate the psyche and to channel libido in service to some value.

~ *Creating a Life*, p. 44

When a person has a powerful reaction to another, positively or negatively, he or she is in thrall to a highly charged imago, perhaps parental, perhaps of a predator, perhaps of an object of desire. We are never without myth.

~ *Creating a Life*, p. 44

What myths are we living? Are we living out our parents' unlived lives, compensating for their fears? Are we in thrall to the values of the herd, which may offend the soul but keeps one compliant company? Are we subject to those splinter mythologies, the complexes, which will direct the rest of our life on automatic pilot for so long as they remain unconscious and unchallenged?

~ *Creating a Life*, p. 45

If myth is the invisible plane which supports the visible plane of life, what happens when the invisible plan is no longer phenomenologically experienced?

~ *Creating a Life*, p. 55

Myth derives from the dramatically embodied imagos which our soul serves, whether we know the or not, whether they are helpful or not, whether culturally imposed or individual in origin. In short, our personal myth is our implicit value system, those internalized authorities and controlling ideas that govern our life, whether we know them or not, like them or not, chose them or not.

~ *On This Journey We Call Our Life*, p. 48

... most of the time one's life serves one's complexes, those deep-seated value systems derived from another time, another place. On any given day, one is more likely than not to be reenacting a mythological system internalized from popular culture or one's family of origin.

~ *On This Journey We Call Our Life*, p. 49

"What is my personal myth?" is of profound significance for it is really asking, "What values, conscious or not, do I serve? What owns me? Of what am I unconscious?"

~ *On This Journey We Call Our Life*, p. 52

Tribal mythologies and sacred institutions have lost their numinosity for most of us. So the responsibility for myth has fallen upon the individual.

~ *On This Journey We Call Our Life*, p. 83

A "mythologem" is a single, fundamental element, or motif, of any myth. The myth of ascent or descent are mythologems. The hero's quest embodies two such mythologems: the hero and the quest, each of which has a discernible lineage and separable meaning, and synergistically enlarge each other.

~ *Mythologems*, p. 7

213

"The gods" here are the personified metaphors of such energies... By avoiding metaphysics we make epistemology possible. That is, by refusing to concretize the infinite in the trapping of finitude, we make it possible to approach the unknowable.

~ *Mythologems*, p. 9

Why use the word "gods" rather than simply "energies"? The reason is that there is still enough potency in that word to evoke respect, and respect is our way of honoring those energies... it is an act of impiety not to remember that all images of divinity are metaphors, lest they no longer be divinities but artifacts of ego consciousness, better known as idols.

~ *Mythologems*, p. 9

Myth as psychodynamic image. An image is a structure capable of carrying energy and, when so charged, has the power to evoke energic response within us.

~ *Mythologems*, p. 10

Myth as personal scenario. While any of us in any moment may be seized by a particular mythologem, we may also come to recognize that we are often bound to life-long scenarios which silently but consistently reveal themselves through the order of our lives.

~ *Mythologems*, p. 10

Myth as tribal value system. The conscious values are embedded in a culture's ethical and juridical systems, its mores and its sense of identity. The unconscious values may be activated by propaganda and advertising, natural or political events, or collective intrapsychic dynamics.

~ *Mythologems*, p. 11

The mythic sensibility is engaged whenever we are brought into relationship with depth, with the autonomous Other, be the Other a person, nature, or even some autonomous part of ourselves which demand the attention of consciousness.

~ *Mythologems*, p. 20

We serve mythology all the time, whether we know it or not.

~ *Mythologems*, p. 57

In sum, the hero is a name for, a designation of, a personification of, a certain energy and intentionality, which lies within us all, all the time, though we may have very uncertain access to it. The hero mythologem is a personification of the energy necessary to serve life's transpersonal agenda, especially its developmental sequence. We are brought here, and every cell in our body knows this, to become, to flower, to flourish. At the same time, there are enormous forces which oppose this development.

~ *Mythologems*, pp. 58-59

Showing up, and dealing with whatever must be faced in the chasms of fear and self-doubt, that is the hero task.

~ *Mythologems*, p. 62

215

. . . the hero task is the act of life risking itself, life as verb, life *live-ing* as it were.

~ *Mythologems*, p. 68

When the inner myth and the outer myth do not line up, then we are divided souls. When the outer myth does not support individuation, then we are living an existential dissociation.

~ *Mythologems*, p. 110

The invisible world governs the visible world, which is one of the reasons why it is so difficult to be wholly, or even partly, conscious. Every life is the enactment of not one story, but many. The story we consciously know, or believe we know, is seldom the whole story which is unfolding within us.

~ *Mythologems*, p. 112

Lastly, the energy at the core of the mythological system is our energy; it is a scintilla of the soul. Whenever it may be assimilated more fully into consciousness, it has the power to enlarge our frame of reference and our scope of action. It is the secret sea from which all our life springs, and without which we are not ourselves. It is our fragmentary glimpse of the gods.

~ *Mythologems*, p. 127

The emergent myth from amid the psychopathology of daily life is already forming in the dream you will dream tonight, in the intuition that comes to you at the hour of the wolf, and in the mystery that is forever renewing itself through the life of each of us.

~ *Finding Meaning in the Second Half of Life*, p. 179

In the face of the exhaustion of the old we may 1) find a higher, more evolved form of the old myth; 2) move to a more compelling myth; 3) live without myth, as one's myth; or 4) begin one's journey to a new place.

~ *What Matters Most*, p. 158

... myth ... an energy-charged image, or idea, that has the power to move and direct the soul....

~ *What Matters Most*, p. 159

Mythic systems, whether tribal, collective, or personal convey images that arise from transcendent encounters— whether with the gods, natural events, the mystery we bring to each other in relationship, or the depths we find within ourselves.

~ *What Matters Most*, p. 159

When we consider that the role of tribal myth was to address four great mysteries, and hopefully connect people in feeling ways to them, we realize how sterile our time actually is. These four orders of mystery, which do not go away, are still being considered by our unconscious, and our felt disconnect from them is manifest in psycho-pathology, sociopathology, mass movements, fads and fashions, and collective projections upon numinous figures who are frequently flooded by that archetypal expectation, as so many fallen pop stars and destroyed celebrities exemplify. These four questions that never go away are:

1. Why are we here, in service to what, and toward what end? (*the cosmological question*)

2. How are we as animal forms, empowered with spirit, to live in harmony with our natural environment? *(the ecological question)*

3. Who are my people, what is my duty to others, and what are the rights, duties, privileges, and expectations of my tribe? (*the sociological question*)

4. Who am I, how am I different from others, what is my life about, and how am I to find my way through the difficulties of life? (*the psychological question*)

~ *Hauntings*, p. 106

As a new myth, scientism is afforded huge latitude of trust and investment, with little thought for consequences or for how we are to respond to the summons to grow up and live with an essential and personal powerlessness before an inexplicable mystery.

~ *Living Between Worlds*, pp. 13-14

Myth . . . represents *the energy-charged values to which we are in service, whether consciously or not, and the goals they serve, whether consciously of not.* Our myths drive us, make our choices, and only a portion of their presence is ever brought to the surface of consciousness.

~ *Prisms*, p. 167

Just as affect-laden images move and shape individuals, so they form cultures, and generate their systems, values, and marching orders. As long as that culture's images speak to the hearts and minds of its members, the myth is living, charged, and links one to transcendent values. When, however, any cultural form begins to lose that energy, no longer moves the heart, it devolves into a concept, a dogma, a set of beliefs and practices, which needs constant reinforcement to compel compliance.

~ *Prisms*, pp. 169-170

Chapter 17

Persona

Persona (Latin, "actor's mask"). One's social role, derived from the expectations of society and early training. A persona is useful both in facilitating contact with others and as a protective covering, but identification with a particular persona (doctor, scholar, artist, etc.) inhibits psychological development.

~ *The Eden Project*, p. 146

The persona (Latin for "mask") is a more or less conscious adaptation of the ego to the conditions of social life. . . Although the persona is a necessary interface with the outer world, we tend both to confuse the persona of others with their inner truth and to think that we too are our roles.

~ *The Middle Passage*, p. 42

. . . a man's relationship to himself, to others and to the life force that courses through him is profoundly channeled by his primary experience of mother. To the extent that she is unable to meet his needs, and imposes her personal complexes on him, so he will suffer the wounds of abandonment and overwhelment. From the former he learns to distrust his own worth and the reliability of the world. Because of the latter he feels powerless to defend his fragile frontier and so evolves a generally compliant, co-dependent personality or a fearful, overcompensated, power-dominated one. In either case, he is not himself, but he lives in reaction to an experience so powerful that it subordinates his natural truth. This compromise formation, repeated through childhood, produces a false personality and furthers the projection of that first relationship onto later, adult relationships. Thus he lives a false self.

~ *Under Saturn's Shadow*, p. 109

Whenever one goes through the deconstruction of the false self, one normally suffers a considerable period of disorientation, of wandering in the wasteland.

~ *Swamplands of the Soul*, p. 38

We become our wounds, so to speak. We live out those reactions which come from the fated wounding and thereby collude with the symbolic expressions. This assemblage of behaviors, attitudes and reflexive strategies constitute our "false self," a provisional identity.

~ *Swamplands of the Soul*, pp. 110-111

I understand the false self to be an assemblage of behaviors and attitudes toward self and Other whose purpose is the management of the existential angst experienced by the child. The development of this provisional personality is inevitable since one is obliged to acquiesce to the dynamics of the family of origin and other cultural forces.

~ *The Eden Project*, p. 29

We know that the infant, and then the child, powerless to enact its own reality, at the mercy of the demands of the environment, both familial and cultural, "reads" the world as a series of messages about self and other and the transactions between. When the environment floods its boundaries, the child learns, irrevocably, its own powerlessness. In service to survival, the adaptive capacity of the child adopts attitudes and behaviors designed to promote survival and enhance the possibility of need gratification. Such a child may organize this provisional identity around the task of gaining power greater that possessed by the environment, by avoiding its demands as much as possible, or, most commonly, seeking to give the environment what it wants in the expectation of reciprocity.

~ *Creating a Life*, pp. 15-16

. . . provisional identity. . . the acquired as opposed to the natural sense of self, as an assemblage of behaviors, attitudes towards self and others, and reflexive responses whose purpose is to manage the anxiety suffered by the child.

~ *Creating a Life*, p. 41

"Who am I apart of the roles I have been playing—some of them good, productive, and consistent with my inner values and some not?"

~ *Finding Meaning in the Second Half of Life*, p. 22

What we initially see in the mirror is what we wish to see, the persona, not the instinctually grounded self. What we are seeing is sometimes called the "provisional personality," the acquired behaviors, attitudes, and reflexive strategies through which we learned to manage the world the best we could. The provisional personality, an interwoven fabric of adaptations, may be far removed from the inherent Self, but, "for good or ill, it brought us this far," so we are afraid to let go of it now. However, life has a way of calling this provisional personality into question. For most of us, this fated encounter is a shocking and confusing appointment.

~ *Finding Meaning in the Second Half of Life*, pp. 66-67

Adaptation to the conditions of life requires the development of a *persona*, the mask we wear in any given social situation. Sometimes we even believe who we really are is contained, or defined, by these personal roles. But the greater the identification with the persona, the greater that the restive dialectic with the Shadow grows. The Shadow— in this case, the unlived life— goes underground and seeks expression through invasions of affect: a depression, for example, a precipitous action soon regretted, troubling dreams, a physical ailment or psychic enervation.

~ *Why Good People Do Bad Things*, p. 55

Given our fragile purchase on the world, given our obdurate dependency, given ignorance of alternatives, given the lack of rational analysis, given the imposing immensity of messages, we all assemble a false "sense of self." Not *false* because we have lied, but false because it is not about us, but always about "them," about "it," about the "other. So we are defined by the other, not from within, not by divine design, but by "the otherness of the other," which we cannot fathom, understand, contain, control, comprehend. So we are defined as *a reticulated network of behaviors, attitudes toward self and world, and reflexive stratagems designed to get our needs met and to manage the anxiety in whose slipstream we daily stride.*

~ *What Matters Most,* p. 8

Our provisional selves, our counterfeit identities, are essentially anxiety-management systems. . . Only when we pay attention to ourselves, our patterns, our painful encounters with ourselves may we begin to discern these alien, implanted "ideas."

~ *What Matters Most,* p. 72

. . . we all, because of our dependency and lack of consciousness, resign our deepest stories, that is, the stories intended by the gods, and trade them in for the provisional stories that our reading of the world around us provides. We pick up the stories of others, we internalize the messages of family of origin and popular culture, and progressively lose the narrative thread of our story.

~ *What Matters Most,* p. 176

. . . we all acquire enormous messages from our environmental settings—family dynamics, religion, education, social contexts, zeitgeist—and all provide compelling messages to serve, run from, or try to solve somehow. All of us internalize these fortuitous events, "message" them, and accumulate a provisional story about who we are and what we are supposed to do and not do. Accordingly, the great obstacle to a satisfying life remains the risky permission to live our lives as the soul desires.

~ *Living an Examined Life*, p. 77

Chapter 18

Projection

Projection. A natural process whereby an unconscious characteristic of one's own is perceived in an outer object or person.

~ *The Eden Project*, p. 146

Projection is a fundamental mechanism of the psyche, a strategy derived from the fact that what is unconscious is projected.

~ *The Middle Passage*, p. 27

Of the many projections possible, the most common are those onto the institutions of marriage, parenting, and career.

~ *The Middle Passage*, p. 28

The erosion of projections, the withdrawal of the hopes and expectations they embody, is almost always painful. But it is a necessary perquisite for self-knowledge.

~ *The Middle Passage*, pp. 31-32

Projections embody what is unclaimed or unknown within ourselves. Life has a way of dissolving projections and one must, amid the disappointment and desolation, begin to take on the responsibility for one's own satisfaction.

~ *The Middle Passage*, p. 34

The more unconscious we are, the more we project.

~ *The Middle Passage*, p. 83

What we do not understand in ourselves is projected onto our surroundings, and so the sum of our society is the aggregate of what is unconscious in each of us.

~ *Under Saturn's Shadow*, p. 27

Yet, surely we are not to blame for having been wounded, for being fragile, for feeling fear. The task of this dismal state of addictions, again, is to risk bearing the unbearable. What cannot be borne consciously will be projected onto a person, a substance, a behavior, and the wheel turns anew.

~ *Swamplands of the Soul*, p. 91

Anxiety which is not made conscious is most pernicious, for we can never know exactly where it will go, and it will always go somewhere—into a projection or into the body. Under the fetid roof of repression breed foul monsters who will, inevitably, break forth from their fetters in some other venue.

~ *Swamplands of the Soul*, p. 107

Only when one has suffered the collapse of projections onto the Other, or tracked the symptomology to its lair, may one begin to recognize the enemy is within, that the Other is not what he or she may seem, and that one is summoned to a deep personal accounting before one can begin to clear the terrain for true relationship.

~ *The Eden Project*, p. 28

Projection, as a psychological phenomenon, is ubiquitous and inevitable. . . It employs multiple strategies, of which splitting, substituting and sublimating are but a few. . . All projection occurs unconsciously, of course, for the moment one observes, "I have made a projection," one is already in the process of taking it back. . . If there is a central law of the psyche, it is that what is unconscious will be projected. This is why Jung observed that "when an inner situation is not made conscious, it happens outside, as fate."

~ *The Eden Project*, p. 35

All relationships, all relationships, begin in projection.

~ *The Eden Project*, p. 36

It is truly frightening to realize how little one is conscious in the formation of intimate relationship, how powerful is our programmed desire for what we have known. What is known is what is sought, even if what is known is wounding.

~ *The Eden Project*, p. 38

What we do not know about ourselves—and we cannot, ever, know much at all—will be projected onto the outer world.

~ *The Eden Project*, p. 45

When we remember the central law of all projection, that what is unconscious will be either repressed or projected, it is clear that a tremendous amount of traffic transpires in any given instant of relationship.

~ *The Eden Project*, p. 48

It is inevitable that projections occur, that transference and countertransference occur, that we have a large project in mind for the Other, for we are never courageous or conscious enough to pull it all back. We remain human in our deep longing for that suprahuman Other. The only question is to what degree we realize this.

~ *The Eden Project*, p. 48

Marie-Louise von Franz has delineated five-fold process of projecting and then re-collecting our psychic fragments. First, a person is convinced that his or her inner experience is truly outer, for it is experienced "out there." . . . The second stage of the projective process arises out of the often gradual perception of discrepancy, the widening gulf between who the Other is supposed to be and our concrete experience. . . The third stage of the projective process, whether in or out of therapy, obliges the assessment of this new perception of the Other. . . The fourth stage leads one to recognize that what one perceived was actually not real, that one was not experiencing the Other out there, but the Other in here. . . The fifth stage requires the search for the origin of that projected energy within oneself. This is to ask for the meaning of the projection.

~ *The Eden Project*, pp. 51-52

Since projections are by definition originally unconscious, we can only withdraw them when we have sustained the suffering of discrepancy. Apart from the pain of such discrepancies, we may detect projections in the same three ways in which we detect complexes. First, there are predictable situations in which complexes, or projections, are likely to be activated. . . Secondly, we may experience projection in a physical way. . . Thirdly, in projection the quantity of energy discharged in always disproportionate to the situation.

~ *The Eden Project*, pp. 52-53

Since the content of every projection is some aspect of ourselves, what we are "seeing" in the Other is something of ourselves. It may seem ludicrous, but in this sense, what we fall in love with is some aspect of ourselves as reflected back to us from the Other.

~ *The Eden Project*, p. 55

This re-knowing, the re-membrance, this re-cognition, is the rediscovery of aspects of ourselves as mirrored by the Other. When the experience is reciprocal, violins play, glowing colors fill the sky, hope is renewed, the world begins afresh. And then begins the process of wearing away the mutual projections. But nothing is more painful than the disappointment of projected hope, nothing is more intoxicating than its arousal. This arousal of hope, this shadowy origin of attraction, is what is called romance.

~ *The Eden Project*, p. 56

Ultimately, the health and scope of any intimate relationships will depend on each party's willingness to assume responsibility for that vertical axis, the relationship to one's own unconscious material. . . The chief burden on any relationship derives both from our unwillingness to assume responsibility and from the immensity of the project. It takes great courage to ask this fundamental question: "What am I asking of this Other that I ought to be doing for myself?" . . . If am expecting the Other to be the good parent and take care of me, then I have not grown up. If I am expecting the Other to spare me the rigor and terror of living my own journey, then I have abdicated from the chief task and most worthy reason for my incarnation on this earth.

~ *The Eden Project*, p. 57

Of every projection we must ask, "What does this say about me?" And what we are asking of the Other, we are obliged then to ask of ourselves.

~ *The Eden Project*, p. 57

Since all relationships begin in projection, the course of any relationship involves the progressive erosion of projection, with concomitant surprise, confusion, dismay, and sometimes anger. . . As projections erode, each party may easily fall into the problem of power. Actually, power itself is not a problem; in and of itself, it is only the exchange or expression of energy. It becomes problematic when it is usurped by a complex.

~ *The Eden Project*, pp. 66-67

. . . one can achieve no higher or better relationship with the Other than one has achieved with oneself.

1. What we do not know about ourselves (the unconscious project), or will not face in ourselves (the shadow), will be projected onto the Other.

2. We project our childhood wounding (personal pathology), our infantile longing (the narcissistic going home agenda), and our individuation imperative onto the Other.

3. Since the Other cannot, and should not, bear responsibility for our wounds, our narcissism or our individuation, the projection gives ways to resentment and the problem of power.

4. The only way to heal a faltering relationship is to render our going home project conscious and take personal responsibility for our individuation.

~ *The Eden Project*, p. 74

Whatever is true to consciousness is compensated by its opposite in the unconscious. The more pious I am outwardly, the more violence lurks in my psyche, for I am the carrier of nature. . . Consciousness . . . tends to privilege one value and exclude its contrary. The contrary does not go away; it is projected unto others, or it goes into the unconscious, only to emerge in some other time and place.

~ *Creating a Life*, p. 104

Projection is invariably present in all new moments, for we seek to understand the new, to manage it, by what we have known of the old.

~ *On This Journey We Call Our Life*, p. 116

A projection rises from a neglected but dynamic value within us; usually it is essentially unconscious, but has a certain energy, which, when we have not attended it consciously, escapes repression and enters the world as a hope, a project, an agenda, a fantasy, or a renewal of expectation.

~ *Finding Meaning in the Second Half of Life*, p. 78

What is unconscious, charged with meaning, has a dynamic autonomy, and is denied inwardly will appear in some guise in our external environment.

~ *Finding Meaning in the Second Half of Life*, p. 78

Our projections arise from issues, values, tasks we have not yet made conscious, so they spontaneously arise from the unconscious and enter the world in seductive ways.

~ *Finding Meaning in the Second Half of Life*, p. 79

Projections always pass through five identifiable stages. At the onset they feel magical; they literally alter our sense of reality and have a compelling power over us. . . the second stage begets disillusionment. The other is not behaving or producing as we prefer. . . thirdly, we begin to do what we can to reinforce the projection, to recover its pristine attraction. . . The fourth stage is to suffer the withdrawal of the projection. . . The fifth stage . . . is to become conscious that a projection has occurred.

~ *Finding Meaning in the Second Half of Life*, pp. 79-80

Being accountable for the content and issues embodied in our eroded projections is probably the chief service we can bring to our jobs, our partners, our children. As we lift the burden of our unconscious traffic off the other, we free them to be whatever or whomever they are meant to be when we are not interfering with them.

~ *Finding Meaning in the Second Half of Life*, pp. 81-82

At least two psychodynamic stratagems are presents in all relationships, at all times, though in varying degrees, namely *projection* and *transference*....

~ *Finding Meaning in the Second Half of Life*, p. 106

All relationships begin in projection. . . one of the ways in which we are able to function without having to reinvent ourselves over and over is to reflexively impose past experience, agenda, and understanding onto each new person, each new situation. These are projections.

~ *Finding Meaning in the Second Half of Life*, p. 106

. . . we have a tendency to transfer those historical patterns. and their predictable outcomes, into every new relation-ship. . . As one has experienced the primal relationships of childhood, so those core ideas and reflexive strategies, with their predictable outcomes, are brought into the present.

~ *Finding Meaning in the Second Half of Life*, p. 107

What is projected and transferred most is our *intrapsychic imago* as charged and programmed by our history. An imago is a very deeply charged image. An image becomes an imago when it activates an archetypal energy field, and thereby touches not just this present occasion, but activates our whole history as well.

~ Finding Meaning in the Second Half of Life, p. 108

Behind our projection is, surprise, surprise, a mere human being like us. Whoever they are, whatever they are, their imperfect reality will inevitably wear through the projection until a different picture emerges.

~ Finding Meaning in the Second Half of Life, p. 113

What we do not know can and will undermine the presumptions of conscious life, and will provide the content of the projection.

~ Finding Meaning in the Second Half of Life, p. 114

We project our inner life, or aspects of it, onto others, onto groups, onto nations. . . Thus that which we cannot, or will not, face in ourselves, or that which disturbs the picture we hold of ourselves, is frequently distanced from the nervous ego by the dissociative mechanism of projection.

~ Why Good People Do Bad Things, p. 16

... so often the one who receives the Shadow projection of others ... will be vilified, crucified, marginalized, gassed, burned, or ignored. *They are the carrier of our secret life, and for this we shall hate them, revile them, and destroy them, for they have committed the most heinous crime. They remind us of some aspect of ourselves we cannot bear to see.*

~ Why Good People Do Bad Things, p. 18

Becoming psychological requires that we continuously reflect on the twin dynamics that are forever at work beneath the surface of all relationships, namely, *projection and transference.*

~ *Why Good People Do Bad Things*, p. 103

Projections are aspects of our unconscious, so we do not know that we have projected an aspect of the soul on such inanimate objects. After all, if people can project their soul onto flags, oaths, institutions, causes, heroes, or celebrities, why not onto money?

~ *What Matters Most*, p. 32

Only after it [occurrence of a projection] has painfully dissolved may we begin to recognize that we placed such a large agenda on such a frangible place, that we asked too much of the beloved, of others, or institutions, perhaps of life itself.

~ *What Matters Most,* p. 149

All relationships, *all relationships,* involve two elemental psychological mechanisms at all times: *projection* and *transference.* The only question is the degree to which these mechanisms operate unconsciously and, as a result, make us do certain things or keep us from doing certain things.

~ *Hauntings*, p. 57

Accordingly, virtually all adult relationships are ghostly reenactments of earlier times and places, earlier personae, and earlier scripts.

~ *Hauntings*, p. 58

A projection occurs when activated unconscious content leaves us and enters the world. When that energy falls upon another person, institution, or situation, we begin to relate to that other through the valences and expectations of our unconscious content.

~ *Hauntings*, p. 85

What I fail to recognize within me will sooner or later meet me in the outer world through whatever projections I have upon the outer. . . what I refuse to face within myself will meet me in the exterior world through you, not as you are, but as I have so construed you.

~ *Hauntings*, p. 113

A projection is a mechanism whereby our psychological contents leave us and enter the world seeking an object—a person, an institution, a role—upon which to fasten. Because this occurs unconsciously, we then respond to the other as if we know it, rather than its refracted distinction. Similarly, we transfer to that other—person, institution, role—our personal history in regard to that kind of experience. . . In re-evoking our earlier experiences, we unwittingly diminish our adult capacity and present interests by approaching the new moment with avoidant, controlling, or compliant behaviors from our past.

~ *Living an Examined Life*, pp. 9-10

It is central dynamic of the human psyche that the less we know of an object, a person, a situation, a context, the more we are flooded with projections. Projections are our way of trying to finesse the vacuum of ignorance, make sense of it, and bring to bear whatever strategies our history has taught us.

~ *Prisms*, p. 29

Projection means I am always dealing with aspects of myself "out there," on the Other.

~ *Prisms*, p. 29

Chapter 19

Psyche and Soul

To understand what it means to be human obliges a growing awareness of the deepest designs of the soul.

~ *Tracking the Gods*, p. 47

. . . as a person disconnects from unwanted aspects of the psyche, so he or she will be at the mercy of their revenge.

~ *Tracking the Gods*, p. 67

The task of healing is an alchemical work. . . Soul work is mythwork.

~ *Tracking the Gods*, p. 149

It is in the swamplands where soul is fashioned and forged, where we encounter not only the *gravitas* of life, but its purpose, its dignity, and its deepest meaning.

~ *Swamplands of the Soul*, p. 9

In the end, we must recognize that just as there is a pool of sadness in everyone, so there is a mountain of anger. Anger is a legitimate reaction of the soul to its wounding.

~ *Swamplands of the Soul*, p. 99

In time, the acceptance of our periodic descent into the underworld moves us toward that enlargement of soul, that embrace of the polarities of life which we call wisdom. We learn knowledge; we cannot learn wisdom. Wisdom arises through the assimilation of suffering. Suffering assimilated enlarges the personality, brings amplitude to the soul.

~ *Swamplands of the Soul*, p. 125

Jungians view the psyche not as a monarchy, as the ego would have it, or even as a central intelligence agency, but rather as an entity that is polyfaceted, polymorphous, polysemous, polytheistic. So there so many voices, many intimations, many directives, some heard, some not, but all persuasive.

~ *The Eden Project*, p. 31

Soul may be defined here as that energy which wants something of us, which impels us to live up to who we potentially are. Its origin and aim are mysterious, but it manifests intuitively, instinctually, in moments of insights. Relationship is sacred as an arena for the enlargement of soul. Our quest for wholeness is archetypal in character, that is, programmed at the deepest level to find meaning in chaotic experience.

~ *The Eden Project*, p. 61

Whoever loses contact with his or her soul is in trouble.

~ *The Eden Project*, p. 103

The treatment of soul is what heals, finally, whether at the individual or the corporate level.

~ The Eden Project, p. 113

For us to re-collect the soul, to re-member psyche, we are enjoined to the contemplation of the poet rather than the pathologist and the artist rather than the psychologist.

~ Archetypal Imagination, p. 122

It is part of the fundamental morality of the soul that the high shall be brought low, the low exalted, and all things will abide not in stasis but in dynamic tension.

~ Creating a Life, p. 106

The fundamental morality of the psyche suggests that the moment one is convinced that something is true, then the opposite is already at work in oneself.

~ Creating, a Life, pp. 106-107

Through risk and suffering we may at last come upon those values which bring resonant assent from deep within. Then we have created a life worthy of the soul.

~ Creating a Life, p. 149

. . . we also suffer greatly when we are not living the life which the psyche wishes us to live. Such existential bad faith will always demand some sort of payment—in the body, in our relationships, in our disturbing dreams, or in the burden our children will have to carry for us.

~ On This Journey We Call Our Life, p. 12

So, what does it mean to re-member psyche? To me it means three things: 1) that we recall that we are psyche's being; 2) that we seek dialogue with psyche which promotes healing in ourselves and others; and 3) that something wishes to re-member us.

~ *On This Journey We Call Our Life*, p. 134

Thus, the price we pay for not attending the healing of psyche is that terrible feeling of inauthentic suffering. The price we pay for pulling out of the ranks is guilt. Our redemption lies in bringing renewal, something unique, back to the group. We serve the group best, then, by being who we are, by discovering our uniqueness and sharing it with others. The false self which we were obliged to assemble in the face of the demands of familial and cultural environments never feels quite right. Something is always trying to break through to us via intuitions, symptoms, dreams.

~ *On This Journey We Call Our Life*, pp. 136-137

Re-membering psyche is the task of homecoming.

~ *On This Journey We Call Our Life*, p. 137

Re-membering psyche asks four attitudes or practices of us. First, we are obliged to "read" the world around us with a spiritual eye. . . Second, we are summoned to do our private work of personal growth, and thereby help the world. . . Thirdly, to recall that our life is not a place but a journey, and not an answer but a question. Individuation is a process not a destination. We are not our history, although it is of us; we are the quality and temper of our journey. And fourthly, we must come to bless this fragile life just as we find it, and be grateful for it. After all, it is the only life we have. No matter what the suffering, the senselessness and the angst, there is always the soul and the Self.

~ *On This Journey We Call Our Life*, pp. 138-139

When the soul is not attended, what kind of healing can occur?

~ *Mythologems*, p. 14

As the dynamic principle, spirit is the dimension of psyche which embodies energy.

~ *Mythologems*, p. 32

As the organ of soul, the psyche is carrier of all, everything, and nothing together, origin, end and purpose.

~ *Mythologems*, p. 41

And yet all of us intuitively know what we mean by the word *soul*. *Soul* is the word we use to intimate that deepest intuitive relationships we have had with ourselves from our earliest moments of reflection to the present. *Soul* is our intuited sense of our own depth, our deepest-running, purposeful energy, our longing for meaning, and our participation in something much greater than ordinary consciousness can grasp. *Soul* is what makes us most profoundly human, and unceasingly drives us forward more conscious, evolved engagement . . .

~ *Finding Meaning in the Second Half of Life*, p. 6

Only by attending the wounding of the soul, as well as learning to align our choices with its mysterious correctives, can we actively cooperate with this imperious summons to healing.

~ *Finding Meaning in the Second Half of Life*, p. 9

There is always a "logical" connection between a surface symptom or pattern and a historic wounding to the soul. Even though the external symptoms may seem irrational, even "crazy," they always emanate from and give symbolic expression to the wounding that has occurred. Therefore, we are, paradoxically, obliged to thank our symptoms, for they catch our attention, compel seriousness, and offer profound clues as to the deep will or intentionality of our own psyche. In the end we will only be transformed as we recognize and accept the fact that there is a will within each of us, quite outside the range of conscious control, a will which knows what is right for us, which is repeatedly reporting to us via our bodies, emotions, and dreams, and is incessantly encouraging our healing and wholeness. We are all called to keep this appointment with the inner life, and many of us never do. Fortunately, this insistent invitation comes to us again and again.

~ *Finding Meaning in the Second Half of Life*, p. 21

To engage with the summons of our souls is to step into the deepest ocean, uncertain whether we will be able to swim to some new, distant shore. And yet, until we have consented to swim beyond the familiar lights of the port left behind, we will never arrive at a newer shore. For some the entry is gradual; others are pushed suddenly into deep waters.

~ *Finding Meaning in the Second Half of Life*, p. 25

Companionship, mutuality of goals, sexuality, and supportive endeavors are great possibilities in any relationship, but when we learn that engagement of the soul's agenda is our real task, that this journey is our real home, then we'll see that how we use relationships will either serve, or hinder, that prospect. Accepting the journey as our home will free the relationship to serve the agenda of life, the agenda of growth, and the agenda of the soul. When we have accepted this journey, truly accepted it, we will be flooded with a strong, supportive energy that carries us through all the dark places. For this energy we have an appropriate word. It is called *love*. It is love not only of the other, but love of this life, this journey, and love of this task of soul.

~ *Finding Meaning in the Second Half of Life*, p. 126

Of every family we must ask, "How well did the soul flourish here; how much life was lost through the failure of modeling a larger life, granting permission to follow one's own course, or was constricted by the glass ceiling of familial fears and limitations?"

~ *Finding Meaning in the Second Half of Life*, p. 131

Doubt is unsettling to the ego, and those who are drawn to ideologies that promise the dispelling of doubt by proffering certainties will never grow. In seeking certainty they are courting the death of the soul, who nature is forever churning possibility, forever seeking the larger, forever riding the melting edge of certainty's glacier.

~ *Finding Meaning in the Second Half of Life*, p. 219

...we need questions that ask that we grow up

- What has brought you to this place in your journey, this moment in your life?

Consciousness is a task that renews its challenge every morning.

- What gods, what forces, what family, what social environment, has framed your reality, perhaps supported, perhaps constricted it?
- Whose life have you been living?
- Why, even when things are going quite well, do things feel not quite right?
- Why does so much seem a disappointment, a betrayal, a bankruptcy of expectations?

...we can spend decades climbing the ladder, only to realize too late that we have placed it against the wrong wall.

- Why do you believe that you have to hide so much, from others, from yourself?

Who among us did not learn to conceal, having first learned that to reveal is to be at risk?

What once passed for amiability, for a cooperative spirit, for "niceness," becomes in the second half of life, an unacceptable liability.

- Why does life seem a script written elsewhere and you barely consulted, if at all?

- Why have you come to this book, or why has it come to you, now?

We all had the sense of who we were for a short time in childhood, and then it got lost. It is possible to get it back and to live a larger life if we are humble enough to confess that what we have been doing with our lives has not proved sufficient. The loss of alignment with the soul is both the origin of suffering and the invitation to its redemption.

- Why does the idea of your *soul* trouble you, *and* feel familiar as a long-lost companion?

The soul is the archetype of meaning and the agent of organic wholeness.

- Why is the life you are living too small for the soul's desire?
- Why is now the time, if ever it is to happen, for you to answer the summons of the soul, the invitation to the second, larger life?

We live amid politicians and theologians who infantilize us by fear-mongering, and scientists and psychologists who trivialize life by addressing only what can be empirically verified.

~ *Finding Meaning in the Second Half of Life*, pp. 238-257

The soul asks each of us that we live a larger life.

~ *Finding Meaning in the Second Half of Life*, p. 260

Depth psychology discovered that our psyche is composed of an infinite number of such discrete energies, some organized around a particular experience, forming a "complex," and others enacting an agenda to meet our needs or avoid presumed harm.

~ *Why Good People Do Bad Things*, p. 29

We are not unitary; we are a multiplicity.

~ *Why Good People Do Bad Things*, p. 29

… when one loses contact with the soul, something pathologizes—some disturbance shows up in one's health, one's relationships, or one's emotional eruptions.

~ *Why Good People Do Bad Things*, p. 120

The psyche embodies the totality of our being: brain, blood, bone, cerebration, affect, and desire. It is who we are, though we can know ourselves partially through the limited purview of consciousness.

~ *What Matters Most*, p. 8

Thus psyche speaks, not with tongues of angels, but with sounding brass, and battens our brain and pummels our person till we collapse and open the door. Then begins the healing; then begins the recovery of what was lost by the necessary adaptations; then begins the wisdom of asking what *really matters most.*

~ *What Matters, Most*, p. 9

Soul, the literal translation of the Greek word *psyche,* is inherently indefinable but is a word, a metaphor, to describe what we consider to be our essence. It is energy that blows through us, that enters us at birth, animates our journey, and then departs, wither we know or not, at our passing. . . so the "soul" is the organ of "meaning." When life is lived in accord with the psyche's intent, we experience inner harmony, supportive energy, feeling confirmation, and we experience our lives as meaningful.

~ *What Matters, Most*, pp. 34-35

Maybe all of us will learn to grapple with the paradox that living out our lives more fully is not narcissism, but service to the world where we bring a more fully achieved gift to the collective. We do not serve our children, our friends and partners, our society by living partial lives, and being secretly depressed and resentful. We serve the world by finding out what feeds us, and, having been fed, then share our gift with others.

~ *What Matters Most*, p. 40

Healing, satisfaction, and meaning only come when we identify what feeds our soul, and find also the courage and the wherewithal to make it happen.

~ *What Matters Most*, p. 41

Healing our souls requires tracking the movement of Eros in our projections onto others, or perhaps tracing the faded footsteps of Eros to the bottom of our depressions, where Eros awaits reunion with us.

~ *What Matters Most*, p. 58

Sooner or later, a great distress will rise from our soul to trouble us, perplex us, dismay us, but which, if we can

251

possibly query it to find what it wants from us, will prove to be our best friend.

~ *What Matters Most,* p. 66

Psyche knows, and will not forever tolerate our abuse of it.

~ *What Matters Most,* p. 67

In choosing security over growth, we all outrage the soul, and the soul, outraged, manifests in symptoms—depression, anxiety disorders, envy and jealously of others, dependencies, and so many others.

~ *What Matters Most,* p. 87

. . . from the psychodynamic perspective, we consider symptoms messages, expressions of the psyche's dismay at our lives, our choices, our values. . . Symptoms invite us to reconsider our maps, revisit the terrain, revision our journeys, and reconsider our purposes.

~ *What Matters Most,* p. 151

I also know that our psyches will not be mocked and that somewhere deep within something profound gets wounded and ultimately reaches the surface as symptoms, projection, obsession, or some form of pathology.

~ *What Matters Most,* p.175

. . . we can say that a central principle of psychic life is: *Whatever is excluded from our psychic reality will go underground as pathological grieving, namely, depression, or will enter the world via projection, and seduce and enslave us with futile efforts to capture and hold finally what forever eludes our grasp.*

~ *What Matters Most*, p. 182

The requirement that we restore psyche to psychology obliges us to enter the inner life in order to better understand and order the outer life.

~ *Hauntings*, p. 20

Again, recall that our psyche metaphorically is an analogue computer, asking have I been here before, what is the message of that experience, and what is my best course of action here?

~ *Hauntings*, p. 55

The human psyche is so vast, and the ego frame so small, that we can never know ourselves fully.

~ *Hauntings*, p. 84

The good news is that the desires of the psyche never really go away. The very presence of psychopathology, or symptoms, are expressions of the will of desire to be heard through whatever twists and torques it must undergo to reach the surface.

~ *Hauntings*, p. 130

All of us fail in so many ways to show up, to step into the largeness of the soul.

~ *Hauntings*, p. 140

The greatest haunting we all suffer is the lost relationship to the soul.

~ *Hauntings*, p. 140

Beware of those who offer answers. They may be sincere, but their answers are not necessarily yours, Adaptive loyalty to what we have received from our environment may prove to be an unconscious subversion of the integrity of the soul.

~ *Living an Examined Life*, p. 4

... the psychodynamic understanding of symptom, dreams, and behavioral patterns is rather to ask: Why have you come? What is it you are protesting? What is the desire of the soul (as opposed to the desires of my environment, my complexes, my history)? These questions do not bury the issue, try to bypass it, or medicate it into numbness, but rather approach the soul with dignity and ask, as we might of any stranger who knocks unbidden at our door, "Why have you come? What do you want? How might we converse?"

~ *Living an Examined Life*, p. 18

Few of us realize that *it not what we do but what we are in service to inside that makes all the difference.*

~ *Living an Examined Life*, p. 20

How do we know what is right for us? Well, the body knows, our deepest feeling knows, and the psyche knows, and each expresses it opinion, even as we learned early in life to evade these continuous messages from our depths.

So, the recovery effort must typically begin with the experience of inner discord, outer conflict, and sometimes heartache and loss.

~ Living an Examined Life, pp. 22-23

We have made enough excuses in our lives, offered enough rationalizations, and evinced enough evasions, but something inside persists, shows up, troubles sleep, and asks more of us—and sooner or later we all have an appointment with our soul. Whether we show up, remember the divine task, remains to be seen.

~ Living an Examined Life, p. 43

A very effective instrument when in the face of blockages and difficult choices is to ask the very pragmatic questions: "Does this choice enlarge me or diminish me?" . . . We should choose the path of enlargement, not in service to wealth, power, fame, or the accolades of others, because it is what is asked of us by the soul. When we choose the small, we don't have to step into the large, which is quite comforting until we realize we are living small, diminished lives.

~ Living an Examined Life, p. 45

. . . it is a violation of our souls if we live our lives governed by our fears. Ultimately, to step into the large, we have to go *through* our fears.

~ Living an Examined Life, p. 48

There is something in all of us that longs for a bigger picture. Something in us wishes for connection, wishes to reframe the trivial in our daily lives, the pettiness with which most of our systems operate.

~ *Living an Examined Life*, p. 66

... most people lack elemental permission to be who they are or to give voice to the magnitude of soul that exists within them.

~ *Living an Examined Life*, p. 78

There is something in us, all of us, that knows what is right for us, which path is ours and not someone else's, something that pushes us beyond our comfort zone into areas of growth, development, and presence in this world greater than we have lived up to this point.

~ *Living an Examined Life*, p. 92

...we seek distraction from the terrible longing the soul feels for connection with the mystery of being here.

~ *Living Between Worlds*, p. 11

Over time, Jung concluded that there was within each of us a deep resilience guided by some locus of knowing, independent of ego consciousness; a center that produces our dreams to correct us, symptoms to challenge us, and visions to inspire us. His was not an amateur's trust in impulse of a captivation by psychological complex; it was a long, patient, humbling attendance upon the *psyche*, or *soul*, and its perspicacious permutations.

~ *Living Between Worlds*, p. 17

Depth psychology recognizes that the presence of symbols—the depression, the anxiety disorder, the self-medication—is a natural expression of the psyche, a commentary on how our life is going from the soul's perspective. . . Thus, we are summoned to ask other questions:

- Why has this symptom come to me?
- What does it want from me?
- What correctives to my course must I consider?

~ *Living Between Worlds*, p. 24

Often, in the place of wounding, our greatest insights, our developed talents, our compensatory energies emerge out of psyche's resources.

~ *Living Between Worlds*, p. 97

Our soul often has high desires, and we have petty offerings in return. The costs slowly mount, and the unlived life slips slowly into the shadowy areas of the room.

~ *Prisms*, pp. 39-40

The thing I fear is my greatest challenge, and the fear I push through is an aperture into the larger life my soul demands.

~ *Prisms*, p. 43

Bluntly put, for every outer decline, failure of powers, environmental constriction, *something within is challenged to grow apace.* Amid the wreckage of history, the carnage of loss, the growing catalog of grief, soul is summoned to grow.

~ *Prisms*, p. 187

Chapter 20

Religion and Spirituality

Fundamentalism is the sin of literalism. It is blasphemous because it seeks to limit the autonomy of divine energy to what can be known and contained. . . The anxiety of ambiguity seeks to limit the autonomy of mystery by fixing the image; the fixation of image is literalism; literalism is idolatry. . . What else is faith, then, but iconoclasm, and the strength to wait upon the mystery?

~ *Tracking the Gods*, p. 10

Perhaps the vital precondition to religious life ought to be the acknowledgement of the primacy of the inner life, the arena in which the God-imago is activated and lives.

~ *Tracking the Gods*, p. 100

A religious tradition severed from its archetypal roots, its mythological grounding, becomes a set of concepts or rituals without depth.

~ *Tracking the Gods*, p. 101

Returning to the source, that is, to the reality of the psyche, frequently obliges the individual to forsake the comforts and certainties of group-think. Such a person must leave behind the collective values of the tribe. Even more, coming into proximity with the source may require the death of the God-images that served one in the past. . . Often a great loneliness comes with the loss of the old certainty, causing many to herd together for protection from the reality of the living gods. In fact, one may observe, without cynicism, that the task of many religious institutions has been to protect its flock from religious experience! If one is not to surrender to the easy assurances of the herd, then, as Jung said, "he has to go on the Quest; then he has to find out what his soul says; then he has to go through the solitude of a land that is not created."

~ *Tracking the Gods,* pp. 106-107

We are now obliged to exercise primary responsibility for our spirituality. Three indices are useful in helping define our relationship to that Cosmic Other. First, there is the principle of *resonance*. . . Certainly the grand religious traditions have preserved myriad images, some of which still carry the energy of soul for certain individuals. Each of us must sort through the magnificent ruins and find those images that speak to us, those that are personally resonant. Activation of the psychic tuning fork within tells us that soul is present. Like calls to like. The principle of resonance tells us what is of us, for us, even as it retains its mystery. No effort of ego, however, can endow an image with mystery once mystery has fled. The second test of our spirituality may be found in our encounter with *depth*. Whatever pulls us deeper into life, even painfully so, opens us to the great life that courses beneath history and below the surface of everyday appearance. The third principle is *numinosity*. When Mystery winks at us, we realize that soul is not only in us, but also in the outer world. That glimmer is the autonomy of soul in the world which seeks to connect with us.

~ *The Eden Project*, pp. 125- 126

. . .the sin of idolatry, arising out of our anxious attempt to freeze, to hold on to, the Mystery.

~ *The Eden Project*, p. 127

There are certain questions we can then ask ourselves in order better to understand our situation:

1. If the central task of the first half of life is to build a solid ego identity, to leave Mom and Dad, go into the world of work and relationship and create a life, then what is the task of the second half of life? What, indeed, is our proper vocation? If the first half of life is about responding to what the world asks of us, then the task for the second half is, what does the soul ask?

2. What is the unlived life that haunts us, summons us, judges us?

3. Where are we stuck in our developmental process? What fears intimidate us?

4. Where do we lack permission to be ourselves?

5. How do we define, practice, integrate our spirituality? . . . Our spirituality is the most critical filed of relationship, for from the quality of our spirituality comes the tenor and outcome of all other relationships.

~ *The Eden Project*, pp. 130-131

We do know, intuitively, the answers to these questions, for all are defined daily by the teleology of our nature. Something in us always knows, though we may not know what we know, may fear what we know . . .

~ *The Eden Project*, p. 131

To live these questions is what will define our spirituality, our relationship to Mystery. We are asked to risk largeness, passion, boldness, loneliness, and finally to risk being what we were intended by the gods to be.

~ *The Eden Project*, p. 132

The core condition of our time has been manifest as a collective spiritual wound. . .

~ *Archetypal Imagination*, p. 14

With the loss of those connective rites and mythic images, the problem of identity and the task of cosmic location, or spiritual grounding, becomes an individual dilemma.

~ *Archetypal Imagination*, p. 14

. . . most theologies have substituted the powers of institutions and clerical dogma for the immediacy and idiosyncrasy of personal experience. . . Both psychology and institutional religion have fallen into the shadow problem where fear of the living, dynamic, sometimes anarchic psyche prevails.

~ *Archetypal Imagination*, pp. 16-17

Although we have lost our spiritual connection, we have not lost our spiritual desire. In the same way, although we are without gods, they have not disappeared. The problem is simply that the images generally available to us have lost the power to point beyond themselves and thus connect us with the mystery, although we may cling to those image-husks with fundamentalist fervor to mask our disquietude.

~ *Archetypal Imagination*, p. 19

If we are honest with ourselves, we are obliged to admit that there was no significant psychological or spiritual growth in our life without the experience of suffering.

~ *Archetypal Imagination*, p. 36

... the chief dilemma of our time is the problem of spiritual authority. Namely:

—*by what truths do I live?*

—*by what truths do I understand who I am?*

—*how am I to use my energies during this transit I call my life?*

—*by what points of reference do I make my decisions?*

~ *Creating a Life*, p. 54

Religion for most ceased to be a felt apprehension of the transcendent and became an ideological affiliation, which is why Nietzsche concluded that God was dead. God was no longer a felt experience. God has become an idea, an ideology, an institution, no longer the living autonomous God of history.

~ *Creating a Life*, p. 55

The recovery of spiritual authority in our time obliges resumption of personal access to the gods. We may know we are in their presence, that is, in the presence of transformative energies, when we experience resonance, depth and enlargement through encounter with the numinous.

~ *Creating a Life*, p. 61

The encounter with the numinous is available to those who have learned to listen for the resonance, who have surrendered the appeal of comfort to the summons of depth.

~ *Creating a Life*, p. 61

So, too, does religious fundamentalism insult the worth and depth of the individual, by insisting on black and white values, external authority over internal experience, and moral absolutism as a way to simplify the ambiguities of the world and the profoundly divided character we bring to it.

~ *On This Journey We Call Life*, pp. 51-52

What are my spiritual points of reference? . . . the responsibility for answering this question is primarily that of the individual rather than the tribe.

~ *On This Journey We Call Life*, p, 65

It is no small task to recover a religious attitude when the whole range of inquiry has been contaminated by the shadow problems of fear and power.

~ *On This Journey We Call Our Life*, p. 71

Whenever fear is not made conscious, chances are very strong that the theology, the psychology, the politics will be fear-driven, fear-based, fear-compensating.

~ *On This Journey We Call Our Life*, p. 73

In the face of our fear, we all search for magic: the right theology, the right psychology, the right diet, right mantra, right partner—whatever offers to hold back the night. The desire for magic reflects our desire for instant transformation, for rescue and protection... Sooner or later we must face the summons to grow up. And if we do, we still must do so again every day, for the fear which haunts our condition renews itself every dawn.

~ *On This Journey We Call Our Life*, p. 75

Spiritual integrity obliges each of us to value the primacy of personal experience, for that is how the divinities come to us. If it does not feel right for us within, then it isn't.

~ *On This Journey We Call Our Life*, p. 75

The principle of resonance is thus the private means by which a person may know what works. And no one else has the right to predetermine that person's experience. Evangelical fervor is an imperialist compensation for unconscious doubt, and represents a potential wound to the spiritual integrity of others.

~ *On This Journey We Call Our Life*, p. 77

Engagement with depth requires us to recognize that our contracts with the universe, our slick deals, our rationalizations, do not exist, made null and void by the autonomy of the world. We are asked to experience the profundity of that mystery which both courses through us and animates the world around. This engagement brings meaning and beauty in our lives. It may sometimes bring terror, too, which nevertheless furthers the individuation process whereby we serve the gods by becoming more of what they intended.

~ *On This Journey We Call Our Life*, p. 78

Our souls long for transcendence, for meaning, for connection. This is who we most deeply are. When that need is intimidated by fear, diverted by cultural idols, or projected onto others, something terrible happens to our souls. When we learn to face our fear, open to the universe without defense and follow what beckons, we will find our true spiritual path.

~ *On This Journey We Call Our Life*, p. 79

The flight to angels helps one avoid the commitment to this world, the work of this time and place.

~ *On This Journey We Call Our Life*, p. 131

In the course of our cultural conditioning, including the religious dogmas which may either sustain or contain the psyche's movements, we come to live most of the time out of the top half of our being.

~ *Mythologems*, p. 73

As we know, institutional religion can often be a defense against the possibility of religious experience.

~ *Mythologems*, p. 111

Fundamentalism, be it religious or political or psychological, is an anxiety management technique that finesses the nuances of doubt and ambiguity through rigid and simplistic belief systems. . . fundamentalism is a form a mental illness that seeks to repress anxiety, ambiguity, and ambivalence. The more mature the personality structure, the greater the capacity of the person, and the culture, to tolerate anxiety, ambiguity, and ambivalence that are a necessary and unavoidable dimension of our lives.

~ *Finding Meaning in the Second Half of Life*, pp. 164-165

The living mystery is hardened into a concept, a belief rather than an experience, and loses the vigor of the mystery. Then one is left only with the artifacts of belief (which need repeatedly to be reinforced, as at religious "revivals" or pep rallies) but not the living experience.

~ *Finding Meaning in the Second Half of Life*, p. 173

The recovery of a mature spirituality is one of the most difficult tasks of our time.

~ *Finding Meaning in the Second Half of Life*, p. 182

Closely allied with the task of gaining, or better recovering, personal authority is the task of *discovering a personal spirituality.*

~ *Finding Meaning in the Second Half of Life*, p. 184

A mature spirituality will seldom provide us with answers, and necessarily so, but will instead ask ever-larger questions of us. Larger questions will lead to a larger life. A mature spirituality is critical for the second half of life because if we do not address these questions directly, chances are we will be living in subjugation to received values which delude, divert, or diminish us.

~ *Finding Meaning in the Second Half of Life*, pp. 185-186

It has been said that religion is for those afraid to go to Hell, and spirituality is for those who have been there.

~ *Finding Meaning in the Second Half of Life*, p. 186

Growing up spiritually means that we are asked to sort through the possibilities for ourselves, find what resonates for us, what is confirmed by our experience not the consensus of others, and be willing to stand for what has proved true for us. For this reason, the twin tasks of finding personal authority and finding a mature spirituality are inextricably linked.

~ *Finding Meaning in the Second Half of Life*, p. 186

Dogma serves as a reassuring program of answers to questions that arise: to explain, to communicate, and in time defend the past for the person who did not experience it directly. The dogma itself does not carry the mystery, though it may sincerely seek to sustain its impact. Rituals have the intent to re-create the encounter with the mystery, to summon up the spirits, and hopefully reanimate the original encounter. Through reiteration, however, rituals tend to lose their connection to the primal energy and increasingly become hollow forms. In time, they tend to become rigid, inflexible entrapments of soul rather than summoners to largeness.

~ *Finding Meaning in the Second Half of Life*, pp. 197-198

Upon reflection, three essential points became clear. First, that the eternal questions will arise in quite different guises in all times, and persist in determining the value of our lives whether we are conscious of them or not. Second, that those who went before us experienced profundities in forms that may, or may not, still stir us as well. We owe it to them, and to ourselves, to inquire seriously. And third, that our culture is failing miserably to bring us to those questions, which deepen our humanity and bring worth and weight to our journeys. This last fact constitutes a betrayal of the largeness of the soul, and therefore a deception of in the individual person by the collective.

~ *Finding Meaning in the Second Half of Life*, p. 200

A mature spirituality requires a mature individual. A mature spirituality already lies within each of us, in our potential to take on the mystery as it comes to us, to query it, to risk change and growth, and to continue to the revisioning of our journey for so long as we live.

~ *Finding Meaning in the Second Half of Life*, p. 206

We need to always distinguish *pain* from *suffering*. Pain is physiological and should always be alleviated when possible, for pain can erode the spirit's vitality. Suffering is spiritual, for it inevitably raises questions of meaning.

~ *Finding Meaning in the Second Half of Life*, p. 210

Without journey, risk, conflict, we are already spiritually dead and are simply waiting for the body to drop away as well.

~ *Finding Meaning in the Second Half of Life*, p. 211

Wherever certainty is brandished so vehemently, it is generally in compensation for unconscious doubt. Our anxieties lead us to grasp at certainties. Certainties lead to dogma; dogma leads to rigidity; rigidity leads to idolatry; idolatry always banishes the mystery and thus leads to spiritual narrowing. To bear the anxiety of doubt is to be led to openness; openness leads to revelation; revelation leads to discovery; discovery leads to enlargement.

~ *Finding Meaning in the Second Half of Life*, p. 220

Central to religious insight, to religious experience, and to psychological awareness is the conscious recognition and acknowledgement of one's limits, to know that we do not know.

~ *Why Good People Do Bad Things*, p. 36

Theologies are thus secondary epiphenomenal response to primary phenomena, and they say more about the limited functioning of our ego and the complexes through which experience is processed than reveal very much about the mystery we call *the gods*.

~ *Why Good People Do Bad Things*, p. 168

But the modern ego has not generally proved satisfied by these polyvalent, protean godheads. With the development of the ego through an accretion of consciousness through the centuries, our existential angst has also increased, and our demand for unity, for consistency, and for the predictable order rises apace. We even tell ourselves that monotheisms are superior to polytheisms, that dualisms are only contradictions. But the contradictions of the most theistic positions are then driven underground, only to surface later as troubling paradox, or unacceptable ambiguity.

~ *Why Good People Do Bad Things*, p. 169

Job is the story *not of the Shadow of God, but of our Shadow problem with that mystery we call God.*

~ *Why Good People Do Bad Things*, p. 171

Notice that *the problem of evil is a problem of the human ego, and the imago Dei it constructs.*

~ *Why Good People Do Bad Things*, p. 172

Most theological growth, and all psychological growth, comes from the greater defeating the lesser, often to our dismay.

~ *Why Good People Do Bad Things*, p. 173

In the end, the issue of dark divinity is our problem, not that of the gods. The Shadow problem is ours, not that of divinity... We are also invited to acknowledge and embrace

271

our greatest paradoxical freedom—in the midst of our greatest defeat—that we are not in charge after all.

~ *Why Good People Do Bad Things*, p. 182

This happy-talk theology [of current Christianity] has an immense Shadow, the Shadow of infantility, of wishful thinking, of denial, of simplification of the complex, and most of all, of the absence of *gravitas* that comes to us when authentically in the presence of the mystery. Such popular theologies and psychologies tempt most by offering transformation without suffering, magic without maturation, and not only infantilize the believer, but betray him in the end, for, as most adults know, there is no magic, only real life with its complexities and tenebrous gradations.

~ *Why Good People Do Bad Things*, pp. 199-200

When we consider how a religious idea emerges in the first place, we must recall that it never begins as an "idea." It occurs as a highly charged, affective *experience of transcendence*, and later, much later, becomes an idea.

~ *What Matters Most*, p. 99

When an image wanes in its power to point beyond itself, to summon up a compelling affective response to the original, it evolves into a *sign. A symbol points toward mystery, a sign denotes a content, an "idea."* . . . three forms whose purpose is to retain access to, transmit the meaning of, and bind the community to its original encounter and its communal meaning. These three retentive forms are *dogma, rites, and cultic* practices.

~ *What Matters Most*, p. 100

272

Dogma formulates the questions and putative answers to whatever "meaning" has arisen from or been ascribed to the primal encounter. . . In time, of course, dogma can cease to summon any affect, and then grows dry, sterile, and well . . . dogmatic

~ *What Matters Most*, pp. 100-101

Rites evolve as reenactments of primal experience in the hope of recapturing its original numinosity. They, too, can in time seem arbitrary and disconnected.

~ *What Matters Most*, p. 101

Cultic practices—how we prepare our food, marry, bury our dead, develop ethical and juridical systems, and so on—are means by which one differentiates those who had primal encounters X rather than encounters Y and Z.

~ *What Matters Most*, p. 101

Idolatry occurs when the focus of our affective commitment has shifted from the primal Other to the image itself.

~ *What Matters Most*, p. 104

A spiritual crisis occurs when our identity, our roles, our values, or our road map are substantially called into question, prove ineffective, or are overwhelmed by experience that cannot be contained by our understanding and world.

~ *What Matters Most*, p. 144

Spiritual crises come to us for several reasons. Among them are: 1) trauma—personal or cultural; 2) autogenous swampland visitations; 3) discrepancies between expectations and outcomes; 4) incongruence between map and terrain; and 5) a dystonic relationship between false and natural self.

~ *What Matters Most*, p. 145

In moments of spiritual crisis we naturally fall back upon what worked for us, or seemed to work, heretofore. . . Regression of any kind is just such a return to old presumptions, often after they have been shown to be insufficient for the complexity of larger questions. The virtue of the old presumptions is that they once worked, or seemed to work, and therein lies if not certainty, then nostalgia for a previous, presumptive security. In our private lives, we frequently fall back upon our old roles.

~ *What Matters Most*, pp. 154-155

At the archaic level of our psychological functioning, we often transfer to the universe, the company, the welfare state, the marriage an expectation that will be "the good parent" and will therefore not let us down. Thus, when grief falls upon us or disappointment overthrows our plans, we feel betrayed, picked on, singled out, rather than summoned to a more sophisticated appreciation of the radical autonomy of the universe and the radical contingency of all things mortal.

~ *Hauntings*, p. 92

We project the child's legitimate but archaic need for the protective parent onto the universe and then are surprised when the universe does not comply with our agenda. As a matter of fact, the great anguish of Western Abrahamic theology whether it be Islamic, Jewish, or Christian, rises from this contradiction between the projections of the good parents as omnipotent God onto the universe and the seeming lack of reciprocity we receive.

~ *Hauntings*, p. 93

... the materialist vision of our time leads to this dilemma: *if the numinous is not experienced in the outer world, it will manifest either as somatic illness, internalized pathology, or we will be owned by our search for it among the objects upon which we have projected our existential yearnings in the outer world.* Thus, shiny new objects, seductive technologies, sex and romance, hedonism, self-absorption, and most of all, distraction constitute the chief "spiritualities" of our time.

~ *Hauntings*, p.105

Our spiritualties will be found not in what we profess but in where our energies are most invested most hours of the day.

~ *Hauntings*, p. 105

An authentic journey will ask us to embrace contradictions, suffer ambiguity, and not fall into either-or thinking, which is so characteristic of the immature or frightened mind. A mature spirituality will be one in which we encounter more mystery than is comfortable.

~ *Living an Examined Life*, p. 66

A mature spiritualty does not offer certainty; it offers mystery.
It offers depth, it obliges reframing our understandings, and
it requires growing up psychospiritually.

~ *Living an Examined Life*, p. 67

. . . a mature spirituality will be found in the five following
points. First, it is the nature of the modern and postmodern
world that, like it or not, one now has a responsibility that
was once tribal. . . Second, a true spirituality opens up to
the numinous, a word that speaks to something approaching
us, soliciting our engagement, not willed by the ego. . .
Third, mature spirituality opens us to mystery, which
means certainty is a luxury of the naïve, the frightened, the
obtuse. This means I must live with more uncertainty that
is comfortable, and however unsettled I may feel, to realize
that I have no honest choice but to go on and engage life
and death on their terms, not mine. . . Fourth, a mature
spirituality asks me to grow up. . . Growing up, at the least,
means that we accept full responsibility for our lives. We
are, all of us, still responsible for meeting our needs, not
some magical others, someone who will fix it for us, lift the
burden off us, explain what it all means, instruct us in what
we supposed to do, and if we are really lucky, take care of
us so that we don't have to grow up after all. . . Fifth, our
beliefs and practices are to be measured not by whatever
solipsistic or seductive certainties they offer us, but whether
they open up to mystery, deepen our engagement with the
unfolding of our journey, and require us to grow up, live
without certainty, yet conduct daily life with values that we
do our best to practice.

~ *Living an Examined Life*, pp. 106-107

A mature spirituality will, in my view, be characterized by some basic criteria. . . Rather than provide us with simplistic answers, which certainly might go a long way to assuage the anxieties generated by ambiguity, one's spirituality humbly respects the mystery and confesses that *any understanding of the essential mystery of life that my poor brain and limited imagination can formulate is surely a product of my complexes or my need for "certainty."*

~ *Living Between Worlds*, p. 112

A mature spirituality is one that *obliges me to grow, perhaps to go deeper into life than is comfortable* and demands I live with grief, fear, and limitation rather than inflation.

~ *Living Between Worlds*, p. 112

A mature spirituality is one that respects *the principle of "resonance."*

~ *Living Between Worlds*, p. 112

Just as the "Self" is a transcendent Other to ego consciousness, so the encounter with the "Other" as God is unknowable. This makes "theology," if one thinks it through carefully, essentially untenable. The transcendent Other is that about which one cannot speak for only silence is respectful of the transcendence of mystery; anything short of that is a construing by ego-consciousness and a distortion by complexes.

~ *Prisms*, p. 122

. . . one may be pretty sure we have made the gods in our own image when they seem to hate the same people we hate.

~ *Prisms*, pp. 122-123

If the numinous is not encountered within ourselves, our need for it will somaticize and damage the body, be distracted or anaesthetized by addiction, or will enter the world via projection onto objects of desire, which will then captivate and dominate us through their power.

~ *Prisms*, p. 175

The purpose of a mature spirituality is to live in depth, whether in the venues of loss and uncertainty or those of plentitude.

~ *Prisms*, p. 194

Chapter 21

Shadow

Shadow. A mainly unconscious part of personality, characterized by traits and attitudes, both negative and positive, which the conscious ego tends to reject or ignore.

~ *The Eden Project*, p. 146

Since much of the first half of life involves the construction and maintenance of the persona, we often neglect our inner reality. Enter the shadow, which represents everything that has been represses or gone unrecognized. The shadow contains all that is vital yet problematic—anger and sexuality, to be sure, but also joy, spontaneity and untapped creative fires.

~ *The Middle Passage*, p. 43

The key to integration of the shadow, the unlived life, is to understand that its demands emanate from the Self, which wishes neither further repression nor unlicensed acting out. . . We learn through the deflation of the persona world that we have lived provisionally; the integration of inner truths, joyful or unpleasant, is necessary to bring new life and the restoration of purpose.

~ *The Middle Passage*, p. 44

The shadow should not be equated with evil, only with life that has been suppressed. As such, the shadow is rich with potential.

~ *The Middle Passage*, p. 78

The shadow embodies all the life which has not been allowed expression.

~ *The Middle Passage*, p. 78

A conscious appointment with the shadow at midlife is essential, for it will be operating surreptitiously in any case. We must examine what we envy or dislike in others and acknowledge those very things in ourselves.

~ *The Middle Passage*, p. 79

As painful as the encounter with our shadow may be, it reconnects us with our humanity. It contains the raw energy of life which, if handled consciously, can lead to change and renewal.

~ *The Middle Passage*, p. 85

The shadow represents that part of our psyche with which we may be uncomfortable, or disdain, or that threatens ego intentions, but serves as a split-off part of the soul nonetheless. Working with the shadow represents the only way of integrating it, for what is not integrated will be projected onto others or leak out in dangerous behavior.

~ *Under Saturn's Shadow*, p. 23

The shadow represents that which is excluded from consciousness because it is threatening, painful, embarrassing, or destabilizing. The shadow may be experienced individually or collectively; it represents a wider, richer range of energy that often operates autonomously and invades conscious life in disturbing ways, but which is ultimately necessary for the expansion and completion of consciousness. The shadow has too often been split off in Western thinking and we know, psychologically, that whatever is split off reinstitutes itself through behavioral eruptions or projections unto others.

~ *Tracking the Gods*, p. 33

As Jung once noted, the greater the light, the darker the shadow.

~ *Tracking the Gods*, p. 35

Jung noted that a shadowless person, which is to say one unconscious and highly defended against the shadow, is a shallow person. Most of us were conditioned to be nice rather than real, accommodating rather than authentic, adaptive rather than assertive.

~ *Swamplands of the Soul*, p. 29

When anything, even a good thing, becomes one-sided and excludes its opposite, the demonic enters in. Even goodness can be demonic when we are posseted by it. One thinks of Jung's concept of the shadow as the necessary dark side to every light; indeed, Jung noted, "more light means more night."

~ *Swamplands of the Soul*, pp. 67-68

Perhaps the most functional definition of shadow is *that with which I am uncomfortable in my culture or myself.*
~ *Swamplands of the Soul*, p. 68

It is no accident that sexuality and anger are the most problematic or shadow encounters, for they are experienced by the ego world and the collective, as anarchic, disruptive to social order, outside of one's control. . . All of us have pockets of anger floating about in our psyche, just as we have pockets of sadness and fear.
~ *Swamplands of the Soul*, p. 94

It is not a question of whether the shadow is at work in a relationship, but how conscious we are of it and how deleterious its effects.
~ *The Eden Project*, p. 82

A useful basket definition of the shadow is: that which I do not wish to be, that within myself with which I least desire to associate, that which I find frightening, anarchic, and threatening to my self-image.
~ *Creating a Life*, p. 119

Our understanding of shadow, however, must be broad enough to transcend the common assumption that the word is synonymous with evil.
~ *Creating a Life*, p. 119

. . . maintain a journal on issues such as the following:

1) When Jung said that the greatest burden of the child is in unlived life of the parent, he was pointing toward the power of that repressed material to set the tone and the agenda for our own lives. In general, we seek to replicate those experiences, compensate for them or heal them, or some combination thereof. . .

- In what way am I carrying the unlived life of my parent?

- Where am I stuck, blocked, as my parent was blocked?

- Where am I caught in a compensation which, though it may be productive for me and others, shackles me to the consequences of someone else's life?

2) How am I perpetuating the world view, the strategies, the behaviors of my mother? Of my father? Where do they show up, like unwelcoming flashes in the mirror which show the parent's face shining through ours, or where one finds one's relationship to one's children not unlike the relationship one had to one's parent, or when the intimate relationship seems fatally wounded by inescapable and familiar patterns? . . .

3) Where is the spontaneous child we once were? . . . The cruel hoax of "retirement" is that when one is finally free to pursue one's interest, to experience one's golden years, little has been rendered conscious, or permissible, in order to make such abundant life possible.

4) Where is the unlived life which haunts, or summons, or intimidates you? We have all been called to spiritual greatness. Not the greatness of worldly standard, but the largeness of individuation, the vocation to be who we are, in the particular fashion the psyche demands, at whatever cost my be exacted by the collective. Somewhere, deep inside each of us, is the knowing which knows us, that mystery which seeks us, desires realization through us. . . Fear of the call is a good fear, for it reduces the other fears to their lesser claim on us.

5) Where am I asking others to take responsibility for my life?

6) Each of us lives, in Satre's phrase, in *mauvasie foi* (bad faith), and are summoned to live in *bonne foi* (good faith). . . Living in good faith does not, of course, spare us suffering, mistakes, death and dissolution; however, it means that one has a sense of the rightness of one's journey, with or without the agreement of others. . .

7) What part of yourself do you need to get to know better in order to feel more complete, to have not simply been a visitor here? What agenda is now demanding attention? What growing up do we have to achieve? What security, old identity, relationship, pathology, do we need to leave behind?

~ *Creating a Life*, pp. 120-122

As Rilke observed, we are not yet ready to live the answers. But we bloody well must live the right questions. If we do, we may someday live into the answers, the place where choice and destiny have been intending to meet since before we were born. Such labor in the camp of concentrated shadow work is critical to the enlargement of soul, relinquishment of false identities, unburdening of relationships, and the recovery of personal integrity.

~ *Creating a Life*, p. 122

Simply put, the shadow is everything about myself with which I am uncomfortable. I may not be conscious of my shadow, or I may not wish to be conscious of it. It is that which unsettles me, undermines my conscious values, or would oblige me to confront my values in a more conscious, sometimes embarrassing way.

~ *On This Journey We Call Our Life*, p. 35

The shadow is not synonymous with evil, though evil on personal, collective and archetypal levels are the venues in which shadow most often confronts our conscious hopes for conflict resolution, peace and justice.

~ *On This Journey We Call Our Life*, p. 35

We embody our shadow in at least four different ways:
First, when it remains unconscious it makes choices for us.
Second, we project it onto others and repudiate in them what is intolerably so close to home.
Third, we identify with it and live it out, unable to critique ourselves or the consequences.

Fourth, we admit that that which makes us uncomfortable is, nonetheless, ours, so we grow in our capacity to work with its energies and consciously assimilate them.

~ *On This Journey We Call Our Life*, pp. 35-36

We learn the hard way that disproportionate emotional reactions to small provocations is always the sign of a complex, and often indicates a shadow issue. We examine our mistakes, patterns, disconnections to see where hidden motives may be present. We examine the content and dynamics of failed expectations to see what in our selves was projected onto the other. And we find our shadow frequently waiting for us in our dreams where the ego has no powers of censorship. Repressed energies and hidden agendas which disturb the ego's sense of itself show up in dreams and fantasies and then, once conscious, become a problem for ego to confront. Though we do not create our dreams, it would seem that, in the end, we are responsible for their contents. The first-century Roman poet Terence's observation that nothing human is alien to us remains the best, humbling reminder that what is wrong in the world, wrong in others, is wrong in each of us as well.

~ *On This Journey We Call Our Life*, p. 36

. . . the shadow is nowhere more influential than in our unlived lives. As infants, later children, we learn to dissociate from our natural selves, our best selves, because their enactment is too costly.

~ *On This Journey We Call Our Life*, pp. 36-37

What child has not made compromises to gain acceptance and domestic tranquility? . . . The price of accommodations for acceptance, approval and the management of angst is the loss of instinctual wholeness, that is, neurosis. Our shadow is at the core of our neuroses, which are in large part symptomatic of our estrangement from the Self, our guiding center.

~ *On This Journey We Call Our Life*, p. 37

Seven Questions for Personal Reflection on the Shadow

1. *What do you consider your virtues?* Can you imagine where they subvert your intentions? Can you imagine their opposites in your unconscious? Where do those opposites manifest in your outer life? . . . When virtue, or right intentions, are automatic, we may be sure that the shadow of virtue is present in the unconscious.

~ *On This Journey We Call Our Life*, pp. 38-39

2. *What are the key patterns of your relationships?* . . . where does the shadow manifest itself such as in patterns of avoidance or in repetitions which bring predictably negative consequences? The covert agenda of unmet needs insidiously burdens relationships. Most relationships fail because we ask too much of them. The narcissistic wounds, which are the inevitable result of one's history return as inordinate expectations, inappropriate strategies and regressive scenarios. . . And where truth may not be told, the foundation is rotten. . . Achieving a reasonably healthy relationship requires a modicum of grace and a large measure of willingness to be humbled by one's own trailing

cloud of shadowy material... As long as we are unconscious of the shadowy agenda we bring to relationships, we are doomed to repetition, overcompensation or various treatment plans... We select a person in the secret hope of getting it right this time. But, since in the end we cannot change the other person and can only be who we are, we have only ourselves to call to account when it begins to feel familiar... The only way to liberate ourselves is to discern what our historic relationships were—their dynamics, their scenarios, who we were, who the other was, and how we are still in thrall to forces who origins are past, not current. . . Only through considerable self-knowledge can we make a different choice and change the course of our relational history. Taking responsibility for doing this work is in fact the best way we can love the other.

~ *On This Journey We Call Our Life*, pp. 39-40

3. *What annoys you about your partner?* . . . definition of a long-term relationship is "finding one special person whom you can annoy for a very long time." . . . The more powerful the programming, the greater the likelihood of repetition; the earlier in our relational history, the more unconscious is its shadowy presence... How heroic it becomes—and we may say loving too—when we can acknowledge that what is stuck in our relationships is in ourselves. Such a recognition is heroic because it requires enormous strength to take on the moral burden of one's shadow, rather than trying to convert the other into what we desire... The good news about shadow encounters in relationships is that they

can become sufficiently concretized to make their dynamics conscious.

~ *On This Journey We Call Our Life*, pp. 41-42

4. *Where do you repeatedly undermine yourself, shoot yourself in the foot, cause yourself familiar griefs? Where do you flee from your best, riskiest self?* Our deepest irritant is of course our relationship with ourselves, the one person who shows up in every scene of the play we call life. By the time one has reached midlife, the problem is not our inevitable wounding and disappointments. Rather, it is the fact that we have progressively identified who we are with our adaptations to our environment. . . The price we pay for obedience to unconscious powers is a reduction in the possibility of wholeness. . . While we need to understand the character of our influential experiences and our consequent coping strategies, the whole point is to recover the captaincy of our own journey. If one has a modicum of consciousness and moral courage in the second half of life, then blame, if blame one must, is ours alone.

~ *On This Journey We Call Our Life*, p. 43

5. *Where are you stuck in your life, blocked in your development? What fears block your growth?* We remain stuck because underneath the surface our stuckness is wired to a complex. . . getting unstuck demands that one be willing to bear the anxiety occasioned by the invisible circuitry beneath consciousness. . . Our shadow, then, is found in the collusion with fear and with the self-disabling deals made by the Quisling in each of us. Better to sell out

my country, or myself, than face the threat of my own largeness.

~ On This Journey We Call Our Life, pp. 43-44

6. *Where do Mom and Dad still govern your life, through repetition, overcompensation or your special treatment plan?.* . . They are the ones who taught us how to be, and therefore who to be, for good or for ill.

~ On This Journey We Call Our Life, p. 44

7. *Where do you refuse to grow up, wait for certainty of vision before choosing, hope for solutions to emerge fully formed, expect rescue, or wait for a guru to make some sense of it all for you?* . . . Fundamentalism, be it religious, political or psychological, is a flight from adulthood and appeals to many because life is so scary. If I can turn my ambiguities over to the rigidity of an either/or dogma, turn my choices over to my pastor, therapist or guru, subscribe to a mythos which rationalizes the suffering of life for me, then I will have "happiness." Such happiness, even when it is attainable, is a manifestation of the shadow for it based on the avoidance of the mystery, of the journey, its largeness, and the courage it demands. It is no crime to be fearful, but it is a crime to therefore relinquish control of our journey to someone or something else. The flight from the living gods, those who bring both terror and healing, is not piety. . . When we remember that the shadow is that which I do not wish to be, the betrayal of selfhood is the inability to acknowledge that that which I do not wish to be *is* me. . . The shadow, then, cannot simply be evil, for it is a requisite

for the possibility of wholeness. . . For those conditioned to be reflexively good, or compliant, the flight from the shadow also becomes the flight from one's best self. A shadowless person is a contradiction in terms. . . To the question, then, what is my shadow? We must answer: whatever within us we wish not to face, but which nonetheless carries the germ of our wholeness. . . Where the fears are, is the shadow's dwelling, and it renews its course in our life through sundry disguises such as projection onto others, repression of a vital part of ourselves, or as the narrowing of life—the wearing of shoes too small.

~ *On This Journey We Call Our Life*, pp. 45-47

. . . we seek most to repress what we cannot face within ourselves, hence the importance of knowing our shadow.

~ *On This Journey We Call Our Life*, p. 140

The reclamation of the shadow is the task of the individuating person, for she or he is ethically charged with integrating the split-off parts into a comprehensive whole.

~*Mythologems*, p. 34

. . . our work with our personal Shadow largely defines our engagement with the Shadow at all the other levels. What we have ignored within ourselves will sooner or later arrive from outside . . . like a truck headed toward us in the wrong lane.

~ *Why Good People Do Bad Things*, p. xiii

Most of them [self-help books] fail us because they do not take the complexities of the human psyche into account. They seldom consider that much of what runs our lives operates outside the sphere of consciousness, nor do they acknowledge that we are torqued within by contradictory motives, that some part of ourselves does not wish to enact the agenda endorsed by another part, that for all the attainments of ego consciousness we achieve, there are darker "selves" at work in quite contrary ways.

~ *Why Good People Do Bad Things,* pp. xiii-xiv

It takes a strong sense of self, and no little courage, to be able to examine, and take responsibility for, these darker selves when they turn up. . . *Examining this material is not a form of self-indulgence; it is a way taking responsibility for our choices and their consequences. It is act of great moral moment, for it brings the possibility of lifting our stuff off of others, surely the most ethical and useful thing we can do for those around us.*

~ *Why Good People Do Bad Things,* p. 5

. . . the Shadow is composed of *all those aspects of ourselves that have a tendency to make us uncomfortable with ourselves.* The Shadow is not just what is unconscious, *it is what discomforts the sense of self we wish to have.*

~ *Why Good People Do Bad Things,* p. 9

As an aspect of ourselves, the Shadow will not go way simply from the entreaties of our will, nor will moralistic "right practices" prove a stay against its influence upon daily life. The Shadow leaks into our daily activities and, in fact, is present in all matters, no matter how lofty their tenor or intent.

~ *Why Good People Do Bad Things*, p. 10

The "personal Shadow" is unique to each of us, although we may share many features with others around us. The "collective Shadow" is the darker drift of the culture, the unacknowledged, often rationalized, interactions of time, place, and our tribal practice. Each of us carries a personal Shadow, and each of us participates in varying proportion in a collective Shadow.

~ *Why Good People Do Bad Things*, p. 10

There are four categorical ways in which the Shadow manifests in our lives. They are found when the Shadow a) remains *unconscious*, albeit active in our lives; b) is disowned by being *projected* onto others; c) usurps consciousness by *possessing* us; of d) broadens *consciousness* through recognition, dialogue, and assimilation of its contents.

~ *Why Good People Do Bad Things*, p. 10

I. The Shadow Remaining Unconscious
The Shadow embodies all that which is troubling to us—that is, foreign to our ego ideal, contrary to what we wish to think of ourselves—or threatens to destabilize the sense of self we can comfortably embrace. . . Who among us is not needy, vain, sometimes narcissistic, hostile, dependent, manipulative? . . . Is it cynical to become mindful of the

presence of the opposite value in whatever consciousness embraces, or is it a deeper form of heresy?

~ *Why Good People Do Bad Things*, p. 12

Who, in the second half of life, with at least a modicum of consciousness and psychological maturity, does not look back upon the past with regret, some shame, and no little dismay? . . . Coming to accountability for our own history is the first step in recognizing what has hitherto been unconscious, namely, the presence and activity of our Shadow.

~ *Why Good People Do Bad Things*, p. 14

II. The Shadow Disowned Through Projection
Consider the convenience of knowing who the enemy is, always—if the enemy is *there*, then they are not *here*, so I have no burden of consciousness, no obligation of self-examination.

~ *Why Good People Do Bad Things*, p. 15.

III. Possession by Identification
What we have denied in ourselves will nonetheless be visited upon the world, sooner or later. To be possessed by the Shadow is to bring large energy into the world. No wonder it is so often so seductive. . . And none of us are more dangerous than the righteous who uncritically believe they are right, for they are the least capable of knowing the harm they bring with them into this world.

~ *Why Good People Do Bad Things*, p. 20

IV. Integration into Consciousness

Rendering the Shadow more conscious is always humbling, but it is also enlarging, for therein we begin to engage, to respect, and come to terms with our fuller humanity. This enlargement of our humanity will frankly ask more of ego consciousness than lies within its comfort zone, but it will help us grow up. . . As Jung further noted, our task is not in the end *goodness*—for the good we do may just as often arise from complexes or Shadow or have unintended consequences—but rather *wholeness*. Wholeness can never be approached without the embrace of opposites.

~ *Why Good People Do Bad Things*, pp. 22-23

As problematic as this Shadow work may seem, it is the only way to experience personal psychological healing, as well as the healing of personal relationships with others. . . Shadow work that we may flee is nonetheless the path of healing, enlargement, and community reparation at the same time.

~ *Why Good People Do Bad Things*, p. 23

. . . we *avoid, repress, split off, project* onto others, and *rationalize*. These are our elemental, primitive defenses against what seems to threaten our insecure or immature ego. Growing as a moral and psychological being obliges each of us to learn more about our Shadow and take it on in a continuing effort of consciousness and courage.

~ *Why Good People Do Bad Things*, pp. 24-25

What we call the *Shadow*, then, is the sum of all those separate energies that operate unconsciously and therefore autonomously, or that are an affront to what we consciously wish to think of ourselves.

~ *Why Good People Do Bad Things*, p. 30

. . . the Shadow embraces *all that we do not wish to be.*

~ *Why Good People Do Bad Things*, p. 39

. . . it is exceedingly difficult for us to acknowledge, work with, and own our Shadow material. The weaker one's ego, the less likely one is to do this work, and therefore the Shadow energies are pathologized by going underground. Being repressed, they can only bubble up in some unexpected moment or venue, through projection onto others, or by subtly taking possession of us and playing out in embarrassing or destructive ways.

~ *Why Good People Do Bad Things*, p. 40

The Shadow is not sex; but its excessive importance represents a failed treatment plan for the soul's desire for healing, for connection, for meaning.

~ *Why Good People Do Bad Things*, p. 50

How many of us, arriving at midlife or later, having done all the "right" things, having served the expectations of our family and our tribe, *feel so little at home in our lives? All of that unlived life is now part of the personal Shadow*—that which one learned to keep at bay since its expression might prove costly to one's necessary adaptations.

~ *Why Good People Do Bad Things*, p. 55

Our adaptations lead us to take on the hues, the values, and the reflexes of that environment, and to internalize the messages of family dynamics and cultural milieu. With each adaptation in service to survival or getting needs met, we risk further alienation from our inherent nature. This is the origin of the Shadow problem. The deeper, more obligatory, more divergent these adaptations, the deeper our pathology.

~ *Why Good People Do Bad Things*, p. 60

. . . the functional definition of the Shadow as *that which renders us uncomfortable in confronting in ourselves.*

~ *Why Good People Do Bad Things*, p. 63

. . . the Shadow issue number one is, "That of which I am unconscious, and/or unwilling to face, now owns a part of my life."

~ *Why Good People Do Bad Things*, p. 64

The Shadow issue comes into play when we ask ourselves *what part of our life we are avoiding.*

~ *Why Good People Do Bad Things*, p. 68

. . . most of *our Shadow material will be found in what we are avoiding.*

~ *Why Good People Do Bad Things*, p. 79

When we do not look within, something within is looking at us nonetheless, subtly making decisions for us.

~ *Why Good People Do Bad Things*, p. 82

Wherever we go, it seems, the Shadow follows... Which of us can ever be conscious enough to contain our inherent narcissism and its shadowy agendas, strong enough to acknowledge unpleasant truths about ourselves without repressing them anew, and committed enough to work through them in service to an unencumbered relationship with the other?

~ *Why Good People Do Bad Things*, p. 83

Thus, the Shadow of narcissism haunts all relationships, even the most evolved, and constitutes the ethical challenge of relationship, namely, *"to what degree can I truly love the Other by keeping my own needs from dominating them?"*

~ *Why Good People Do Bad Things*, p. 94

Acknowledging that *we* are the only constant in every relationship requires taking on the problem of our Shadow.

~ *Why Good People Do Bad Things*, p. 98

Repressing what is natural within us breeds monsters sooner or later. The most common monster will be depression, the sort of depression that comes from our own psyche's protest at our abdication. The next most common monster will be anger, the secondary response to the anxiety begun in the denial of legitimate self-interest.

~ *Why Good People Do Bad Things*, p. 98

None of us is free of the deep, archaic fantasy that the other will make our life work for us, offer meaning, bring relief to prior wounds, and, if we are lucky, spare us the burden of growing up and taking our own life on. The Shadow task here is daunting, for it means that one has to step into places of doubt and anxiety, one has to accept a larger definition of oneself, and one has to accept finally that we are all alone, radically alone, and never more so than when in relationship with another.

~ *Why Good People Do Bad Things*, p. 100

My capacity to tolerate myself, when I am really present to myself, forecasts my capacity to be in a nonaggressive, non-narcissistic relationship to the other. What a strange paradox this is, then, that *the Shadow summons of tolerating ourselves is directly linked to the Shadow challenge of tolerating the otherness of the Other.*

~ *Why Good People Do Bad Things*, p. 101

Everywhere we move, our Shadow trails us—its hidden agendas, its repressed motives, its imposing history, its unlived life, its fear-driven stratagems.

~ *Why Good People Do Bad Things*, p. 108

That of which we are unconscious, or unwilling to face, will contribute to our collective, institutional Shadow.

~ *Why Good People Do Bad Things*, p. 131

Where is light is greatest, the Shadow is longest.

~ *Why Good People Do Bad Things*, p. 135

Whether the institution is a corporation, a religious academic, or charitable body, or a government, it has its own limited vision and always begets a Shadow agenda and a Shadow cost.

~ Why Good People Do Bad Things, p. 138

Our proclivity to routinely presume our purity of motive, certainty of outcome, and high-minded agenda is often undercut by a later recognition of hidden causes and unexpected outcomes.

~ Why Good People Do Bad Things, p. 152

How much easier it is to demonize our neighbor than to see the darkness within ourselves?

~ Why Good People Do Bad Things, p. 155

In our Shadow life, we are more fully human—that is, embodying more fully whatever the gods intended by our diverse possibilities. Only the conventional ego thinks it is supposed to be rational, predictable, manageable.

~ Why Good People Do Bad Things, p. 163

Nothing is as powerful as an idea that allows us to justify our complexes, our hidden agendas, our self-interest.

~ Why Good People Do Bad Things, pp. 164-165

When we remember that the simplest, most functional definition of the Shadow is *that which renders us uncomfortable with ourselves*, then we realize the authentic, less adapted parts of us may challenge and even threaten the ego but remain who we really are, and insist of coming into expression through us into the world.

~ Why Good People Do Bad Things, p. 185

But this generic issue is common to us all, namely, the recovery of personal authority in the second half of life. The recovery of such authority is critical to the examined life, critical to the recovery of one's proper journey, and is only possible by the reclamation of whatever has been consigned to our Shadow.

~ *Why Good People Do Bad Things*, p. 190

Finding and expressing a personal authority is thus a huge Shadow task in the second half of life, for we have grown allied against our natural, best selves.

~ *Why Good People Do Bad Things*, p. 193

. . . most of us are thus divided against ourselves. So who we are, what we are summoned to incarnate in this world, in the service of the gods, falls into the Shadow. . . Our positive Shadow, like the dark Shadow, is *who we really are.* The Shadow is always an expression of the will of the gods, however uncomfortable that may prove to our nervous consciousness.

~ *Why Good People Do Bad Things*, p. 194

Another Shadow issue that haunts anyone in the second half of life . . . is the problem of self-acceptance, self-forgiveness.

~ *Why Good People Do Bad Things*, p. 195

Yet, is not the Shadow task here precisely self-forgiveness, not denial, but self-acceptance? How can I accept you if I cannot accept myself? How could I ever love you when I despise myself? When I do despise myself is that not an inflation as well? Where is it written that I am to be perfect, that more of me is demanded than my human limitations allow?

~ *Why Good People Do Bad Things*, p. 196

Self-acceptance, then, can be one of the most powerful Shadow issues. To affirm this wretched soul that I am is a positive redemption from the Shadow world of self-estrangement.

~ *Why Good People Do Bad Things*, p. 196

To gain the positive values rising from that "landfill" we call the Shadow, we have to wrestle with Jung's suggestion that to be a full adult, we have to *know what we want* and to *do it*.

~ *Why Good People Do Bad Things*, p. 198

All violations of our nature ultimately go underground and reappear as symptoms—behavioral, somatic, intrapsychic, relational—for what is denied consciously will only hide for a while and then break through again into our world.

~ *Why Good People Do Bad Things*, p. 205

Questions for Shadow Work Reflection
1. Since we all aspire to virtue, or aspire at least to consider ourselves virtuous, *what do you consider to be your virtues? Can you imagine the opposite of your virtues? Can you imagine that they could lurk in your unconscious? Can you see some place in the present, or in your history, where the opposites may in fact be manifest in your life?*

Even our *virtues become demonic when not balanced by their opposite.* . . The opposite of virtue, then, is unconsciousness, which sooner or later begets what we least intend.

~ *Why Good People Do Bad Things*, pp. 207-211

2. What are the key patterns of your relationships? That is to say, where do Shadow issues manifest in patterns of avoidance, aggression, or repetition?

Where we found others most deficient and most neglectful in our history is where we will prove most needy, most demanding, or most manipulative of the one we profess to love.

~ *Why Do Good People Do Bad Things*, p. 213

3. What annoys you about your partner or others in general?

. . . a committed relationship as the act of "finding someone whom you can annoy for a very long time." . . . Shadow work requires a heroic willingness to take responsibility for oneself, to grow up, and therefore be less demanding and expectant of our partners. . . What we hate in the other is what we hate in ourselves.

~ *Why Do Good People Do Bad Things*, pp. 215-219

4. Where do you repeatedly undermine yourself, create harmful replications, produce the same old, same old? Where do you flee from your best, riskest self?

None of us begin the day thinking, "Well, today I shall do the same stupid things I have been doing for decades, but it will all turn out better." Yet, everyday, the complexes, those historically charged energy cluster, operate in their autonomous way, and the same old, same old surfaces. The complexes take over the ego, flood it with their historic scripts, and the familiar, predetermined choices result, even as we believe ourselves free and conscious in any given moment.

~ *Why Do Good People Do Bad Things*, p. 220

5. Where are you stuck in your life, blocked in your development? What fears, what familiar issues block your growth

… we are stuck because the stuck places are "wired" to complexes, energy clusters from our history. Not only do these complexes have a powerful charge of energy and a "fight or flight" plan accompanying them, they are also triggered by multiple stimuli. We often swim in this inner material and do not even recognize it for what it is because the outer situation presents itself as something new, as in fact it is. But we view through old lens, reiterate the archaic patterning process, and impose it anew. . . Pushing back is how we grow up and claim the life we are meant to live.

~ *Why Do Good People Do Bad Things*, pp. 222- 224

6. Where do Mom and Dad still govern your life—through repetition, overcompensation, or your special treatment plan?

As William Faulkner once observed, the past is not dead; it is not even past.

~ *Why Do Good People Do Bad Things*, pp. 215-228

7. Where do you refuse to grow up, wait for magical solutions to the raggedy edges of life, expect rescue, or someone to step forth and take care of it all for you? Where is the guru who will make these choices easy for you?

~ *Why Do Good People Do Bad Things*, p. 228

Sooner or later we are obliged to face this paradox: Since the Shadow is composed of *what I do not wish to be*, my deepest, most refractory Shadow will be found in what I most wish to avoid, namely, *becoming me*.

~ *Why Do Good People Do Bad Things*, p. 232

. . . our Shadow work is an invocation to us, a calling forth, and carries the germ of our possible wholeness. The first place to look for the Shadow is 1) where our fears are found, 2) where we are most ugly to ourselves, or 3) for the many, daily deals we make, the adaptations, and the denials that only deepen the darkness. The challenging paradox remains: We will never experience healing until *we can come to love our unlovable places, for they, too, ask love of us*.

~ *Why Do Good People Do Bad Things*, p. 235

Shadow work requires a discipline, an attitude, a consistency of intentionality on the part of each of us.

~ *Why Do Good People Do Bad Things*, p. 235

Shadow work always challenges the ego, overthrows it, humbles it, sometimes even slays it. That, paradoxically, is its gift, *if* we can bear such a gift.

~ *Why Do Good People Do Bad Things,* p. 237

. . . that we become progressively aware of, explore, take responsibility for our personal shadow. The shadow includes parts of ourselves that make us uncomfortable with ourselves, whether it be our capacity for evil; or insurgent, narcissistic agendas; or our most spontaneous, healing instinctually grounded selves.

~ *What Matters Most,* p. x

We are often called to save the appearances, to paper over the gap between our presumptive identity and values and our actual practices. This distressing gap is what Jung called the *Shadow,* those parts of ourselves that make us uncomfortable with ourselves.

~ *What Matters Most,* p. 25

. . . I would define the shadow as those parts of us, or of our groups and organizations, that, when brought to consciousness, are troubling to our concept of ourselves, contradictory to our professed values, or intimidating in what they might ask of our timid souls.

~ *Living an Examined Life,* p. 91

Learning about and confronting our shadow is a central moral problem. This means that we have to be able to recognize our narcissistic motives, our cowardly retreats, and our slippery deal making with our values and still not be overwhelmed by guilt for our "unlovable" parts.

~ Living an Examined Life, p. 91

Still, is it not the beginning of wisdom to recognize that what is wrong in the world is also wrong in me and that what must be righted in the world begins with me, rather than preaching to my neighbor?

~ Living an Examined Life, p. 92

... the biggest shadow issue, which people most resist, most rationalize away, most avoid, is the magnitude of the unlived life.

~ Living an Examined Life, p. 92

The capacity to love our unlovable parts is not an endorsement but a recognition that they are also part of who we are. . . These unlovable parts are what makes us most human and therefore most worthy of grace and of love. Only grace, which accepts, and love, which heals, can ever lead us to a larger spiritual life, lest we remain mired in recrimination and derogation of the richness of the soul.

~ Living an Examined Life, p. 95

The Shadow represents these elements, energies, and agendas in us or in our affiliative associations that, when brought to consciousness, contradict our professed values. The Shadow is not evil, per se, though much evil derives from it, rather the Shadow embodies the contrarian dimensions of our soul.

~ Living Between Worlds, p. 126

What I am unwilling to face in myself will always be carried by someone else. Perhaps we are only here to help each other get through life. Unburdening our partners, children, neighbors by lifting our stuff of them is one way to start.

~ *Living Between Worlds*, p. 127

The shadow side, or "dark side," is dark not only because it may be (but is not necessarily) the repository of "evil," but also because it is the hidden side—that is, the side upon which light does not fall. It is dark because it is ignored or not illuminated.

~ *Prisms*, p. 129

. . .a shadowless person is a superficial person, a person without values, without commitments, a person governed by chameleonlike adaptation that estrange one from the rich textures of the soul.

~ *Prisms*, p. 129

Most commonly, the Shadow manifests in our personal lives through the *unconscious* as it spills into one's self-defeating choices, one's narcissistic agenda, or even one's unlived life transmitted to one's children, who carry it into subsequent generations. The greatest burden the child must carry, Jung asserted, is the unlived life of the parent.

~ *Prisms*, p. 132

The Shadow is not synonymous with evil, *per se*. It is a metaphor to embody whatever ego consciousness, personal or collective, prefers to disown. *That within me which makes me uncomfortable about me, that which I prefer to repress, deny, discard, is my Shadow.* Accordingly, the Shadow may also embody some of my best qualities, such as creativity, desire, spontaneity—all movement of affect that at some point in our development proved costly or contradictory to the norms of our family or cultural context.

~ *Prisms*, p. 133

The Shadow is *projected onto others.* What I wish to disown in myself I will see in you and condemn it.

~ *Prisms*, p. 133

Often, what we dislike most about others is how they embody aspects of our own Shadow.

~ *Prisms*, p. 133

Chapter 22

Vocation

A vocation is what we are called to do with our life's energy. It is a requisite part of our individuation to feel that we are productive, and not responding to one's calling can damage the soul.

~ *The Middle Passage*, p. 72

We do not really choose a vocation; rather it chooses us.

~ *The Middle Passage*, p. 72

The *vocatus* is to become ourselves as fully as we are able; the task is to find out how. We are judged not only by the goodness of our heart, but also by the fullness of our courage.

~ *The Middle Passage*, p. 74

Each of us has questions to ask and answer in very private ways. Each question serves to stir the sediment below. . . Each question serves to bring to the surface elements of the personal myth, the implicit values shaping one's daily life.

~ *Tracking the Gods*, p. 142

What is your life's vocation or "calling" (as opposed to source of economic livelihood)? When did your childhood end? When did you leave home? *Have* you left home? How do your dependencies manifest? How do you repeatedly hurt yourself, undermine yourself? Where are you stuck in your journey? How are you still carrying Mother, Father? What fears block you? What is the unlived life that haunts you? What, on the invisible place, supports your life on the visible plane?

~ *Tracking the Gods*, p. 142

These questions [see above] are ineluctable, inescapable, imperative for a responsible, conscious life. If not consciously addressed, daily life carries far too great a burden of sadness.

~ *Tracking the Gods*, p. 143

. . . Rilke's vision of why we are here. Put simply, through acts of consciousness, reverence, mindfulness, and speech, we are here to *praise*. We, the most fleeting, bring meaning into the world through the verbal venues of praise. . . Our *vocatus* is to praise and, by doing so, grant things deeper being and bring consciousness to them.

~ *Archetypal Imagination*, p. 50

One is called to live one's values in the world, quite apart from the likelihood of success, validation or self-aggrandizement. The embodiment of one's vocation, the calling to be a person of value in the world, is arguable the chief task of the second half of life. One is generally in service to the world and ego development in the first half, but to be in service to the soul in the second half is quite another matter.

~ *Creating a Life*, p. 94

The shape and character of our vocation may change at different developmental stages. We have not just one life, but many lives to live, and in the course of however long we are privileged to live, many tasks, many vocations. Personality . . . is not found in adjustment to external expectations, but in serving one's calling in the context of our environment. This may bring one to an individual experience of being "misjudged, derided, tortured, and crucified." No wonder vocation is so seldom served. And yet, and yet, something in us always knows better. Something in us, no matter how much we flee it, summons us. We may avoid it all our lives, but deep down, something knows. It knows us whether we wish to know it or not.

~ *Creating a Life*, p. 110

In the end, a real life will have little to do with the plans of culture or ego, but rather will be shaped by what the gods have in mind.

~ *Creating a Life*, p. 111

We will be most nearly real when we serve our vocation. We will not be spared suffering, but we will be granted a deeply felt sense that our life is right, even suffering isolation and rejection.

~ *Creating a Life*, p. 111

The idea of vocation (from Latin *vocatus*, a calling or summons), what one is called to do with one's life energies, is replaced by career planning. . . There is nothing wrong with work . . . but to choose a lifetime's occupation based on a paycheck or future pension is deeply destructive to the soul.

~ *On This Journey We Call Our Life*, pp. 57-58

In different stages of life, our vocation evolves. . . Another way of putting it is that question which the first half of life asks of us is: "Do you have enough energy, courage, resourcefulness, to enter the world, take on its demands, and create your own conscious place in it?" . . . In the second half of life, the question becomes: "Who, now, apart from the roles you play, are you? What does the soul ask of you? Do you have the wherewithal to shift course, deconstruct your painfully achieved identity, risking failure, marginalization and loss of collective approval?"

~ *On This Journey We Call Our Life*, p. 58

The whole second half of life calls us to a spiritual, by which I mean a psychological, agenda, while maintaining one's participation in the social community.

~ *On This Journey We Call Our Life*, p. 58

. . . we are behaviors and cognitions and psychopharmacological processes, but add them together and one still has the mystery of identity, of vocation, of suffering, of meaning. . . How can we not suffer a sickness of the soul when such important questions are ignored? . . . soul questions *matter*.

~ *On This Journey We Call Our Life*, p. 59

Who among us is free of these sorts of deeply painful agendas: that we must gain the love of the other, or keep them at a distance lest they smother us, or use them to stay in control of our fragile environment? Are any of us immune to this common consequence of adapting to the demands of a powerful external world? . . . today I am obliged to believe that they underestimate the seductiveness of the dark gods, their terrible power to insinuate themselves into our lives when we least suspect their presence. How, then, can we choose, if we know not the place from which our choices emanate?

~ *On This Journey We Call Our Life*, pp. 61-62

Either way brings terrible suffering. One is a suffering that authenticates one's values; one is the suffering that comes from living inauthentically. We all know this latter, for it is our common condition, even as the former is our common summons.

~ *On This Journey We Call Our Life*, p. 62

The real choices in life will always involve the conflict between competing values, each of which has some considerable claim on us, or there would be no difficulty in the first place. Usually, upon closer examination, the choices we face require us to leave some familiar stance in life and move into the unknown. Usually they require the acceptance of a greater level of anxiety, ambivalence and ambiguity that we find ourselves comfortable. They require us to grow, often painfully. In fact, that such choices are not easy is a good sign that we are on the right path.

~ *On This Journey We Call Our Life*, p. 63

Even when one finally tumbles to a long-lost talent or enthusiasm, and the supporting energy is palpable, we are seldom spared old issues or diminished permission, uncertain self-worth, lack of models or obstructive fears. Those old Quislings do not go away. They hang around for a lifetime and make trouble.

~ *On This Journey We Call Our Life*, p. 63

In the end, the choice of vocation is also an acknowledgment that *something is in fact choosing us. . .* It is what the gods wish that determines vocation. If we can bear that truth and serve it, then the gods and our vocation serve us, however perilous the path.

~ *On This Journey We Call Our Life*, p. 63

The reciprocity of energy which arises to support us when we are doing the right thing for the soul, rather than the right thing for a parental complex, is validation, even when few things in life are certain. The search for this reciprocal energy may be the contemporary form of the old Grail question, "Whom does the Grail serve?" My surmise is that the answer to the question that was so daunting to many knights and pilgrims is, "The Grail serves who serve it." Thus the real Grail question is, "What am I called to serve?"

The answer will play out differently for each of us, for we each have our own destiny, a separate *vocatus*. But in any case we will be served, in turn, by that which we have been summoned to serve.

~ *On This Journey We Call Our Life*, pp. 63-64

The work we are called upon do is not the job for which we are paid. The work, the *opus*, is the search for the gods, the search for one's vocation, the tracking of the invisible.

~ *On This Journey We Call Our Life*, p. 119

The sham we perpetrate when we insist on our young people preparing for a lifelong career means we wish them to arrive at midlife about as unhappy with their lives as their parents.

~ *Finding Meaning in the Second Half of Life*, p. 144

If our work does not support our soul, then the soul will exact its butcher's bill elsewhere. Wherever the soul's agenda is not served, some pathology will surface in the arena of daily life.

~ *Finding Meaning in the Second Half of Life*, p. 149

We may choose careers, but we do not choose vocation. Vocation chooses us. *To choose what chooses us* is a freedom the by-product of which will be a sense of rightness and a harmony within, even if lived out in the world of conflict, absent validation, and at considerable personal cost.

~ *Finding Meaning in the Second Half of Life*, p. 149

The sense of ennui, restlessness, sometimes even depression that comes with the achievement of one's ambitions, or the failure to achieve them, is the generally unwelcome invitation to disidentify with those goals.

~ *Finding Meaning in the Second Half of Life*, p. 152

Vocation, even in the most humble of circumstances, is a summons to what is divine. Perhaps it is the divinity in us that wishes to be in accord with a larger divinity. Ultimately, our vocation is to become ourselves.

~ *Finding Meaning in the Second Half of Life*, p. 154

Each of us has been enlisted in the fulfillment of our parent's wishes for us, in the proffered security of sanctioned cultural forms, gender roles, and such contemporary values as materialism, self-indulgence, and hedonism. And each of us has suffered, and continues to suffer, for so passively complying. When consciousness is strong enough to undertake the task of submission to and honest dialogue with the soul, then one will experience healing, and know the difference between job and calling, between career and vocation.

~ *Finding Meaning in the Second Half of Life*, pp. 157-158

. . . surely we are called to become more fully what we are, in simple service to the richness of the universe of possibilities.

~ *Finding Meaning in the Second Half of Life*, p. 158

The developmental process that leads to our growth, maturation, and fuller personhood is a continuing *vocatus*, namely, "a call." Rising from deep within us, the call comes to change—to die unto old understandings and adaptations, the old comforts and compromises—and when we resist the call of our psyche we grow sicker and sicker, or more and more depressed, and have to work harder just to stay in place. Accepting the necessity of exile is also to accept the possibility of homecoming.

~ *What Matters Most*, p. 238

Could it be that . . . the summons to live our journey is a *vocatus*, a calling forth, quite separate from one's conscious desires?

~ *Hauntings*, p. xvii

What does it mean to be here? To what am I called? What values, traits, and capacities must I embody in my life? These are the kind of questions that call us out of the trivial, that help us reframe our frustrations and disappointments and step into something larger than fitting in, being successful, being safe, and being accepted by everyone.

~ *Living an Examined Life*, p. 67

Vocation derives from the Latin *vocatus*, meaning "calling" or "to be called." Ego consciousness does not do the calling, rather, the ego, the whole person is called. Called by what? God, nature, the soul? Use the metaphor you prefer. *Called* means that the ego consciousness, fragile and frangible, nervous and driven, fixed or flowing it is in any moment, lives at all hours in a larger context. Part of what it means to be an emergent adult is to realize both the tiny place our ego holds, like a fragile cork floating on a tenebrous sea, and the immense summons to which it is accountable . . . Vocation is our duty to our calling.

~ *Living an Examined Life*, p. 100

Jung's concept of individuation is meant to be seen in this light—namely, as a duty to the soul.

~ *Living an Examined Life*, p. 101

Some measure of suffering is demanded wherever vocation summons a person. For Jung, the idea of individuation is not about ego sovereignty but about sacrifice.

~ *Living an Examined Life*, p. 101

If *healing* is an act of supportive nature, *vocation* is a summons of the soul. . . Each of us must remember that we were sent with the gift of our personhood, and if we fail to embody that in the world, we have failed our mission. . . The work of healing begins by attending to the soul's desire for expression.

~ *Living Between Worlds*, p. 93

Works Cited

The Middle Passage: From Misery to Meaning in Mid-life.
Toronto: Inner City Books, 1993.

Under Saturn's Shadow: The Wounding and Healing of Men.
Toronto: Inner City Books, 1994.

Tracking the Gods: The Place of Myth in Modern Living.
Toronto: Inner City Books, 1995.

Swamplands of the Soul: New Life in Dismal Places. Toronto:
Inner City Books, 1996.

The Eden Project: In Search of the Magical Other. Toronto:
Inner City Books, 1998.

Archetypal Imagination. College Station: Texas A&M
University Press, 2000.

Creating a Life: Finding Your Individual Path. Toronto:
Inner City Books, 2001.

On This Journey We Call Our Life: Living the Questions.
Toronto: Inner City Books, 2003.

Mythologems: Incarnations of the Invisible World. Toronto:
Inner City Books, 2004.

*Finding Meaning in the Second Half of Life: How to Finally,
Really Grow Up.* New York: Gotham Books, 2005.

*Why Good People Do Bad Things: Understanding Our
Darker Selves.* New York: Gotham Books, 2007.

What Matters Most: Living a More Considered Life. New York: Gotham Books, 2009.

Hauntings: Dispelling the Ghosts Who Run Our Lives. Asheville: Chiron Publications, 2013.

Living an Examined Life: Wisdom for the Second Half of the Journey. Boulder: Sounds True, 2018.

Living Between Worlds: Finding Personal Resilience in Changing Times. Boulder: Sounds True, 2020.

Prisms: Reflections on the Journey We Call Life. Asheville: Chiron Publications, 2021.

References

Chapin, H. (1972). Greyhound. On *Heads & Tales.* [CD] New York: Elektra/Asylum Records.

Meade, M. (2012). *Fate and destiny: Two agreements of the soul.* (rev. and exp. ed.) Seattle: Greenfire Press.

Rumi. (2004). There's nothing ahead. In *The essential Rumi.* (C. Barks, Trans., new exp. ed.). New York: HarperOne.

Ingram Content Group UK Ltd.
Milton Keynes UK
UKHW041453040623
422846UK00001B/60